China History

The History of China's Most Famous Landmark

(A Captivating Guide to the Ancient History of China)

Jerry Arnold

Published By **Ryan Princeton**

Jerry Arnold

All Rights Reserved

China History: The History of China's Most Famous Landmark (A Captivating Guide to the Ancient History of China)

ISBN 978-1-77485-576-8

No part of this guidebook shall be reproduced in any form without permission in writing from the publisher except in the case of brief quotations embodied in critical articles or reviews.

Legal & Disclaimer

The information contained in this ebook is not designed to replace or take the place of any form of medicine or professional medical advice. The information in this ebook has been provided for educational & entertainment purposes only.

The information contained in this book has been compiled from sources deemed reliable, and it is accurate to the best of the Author's knowledge; however, the Author cannot guarantee its accuracy and validity and cannot be held liable for any errors or omissions. Changes are periodically made to this book. You must consult your doctor or get professional medical advice before using any of the suggested remedies, techniques, or information in this book.

Upon using the information contained in this book, you agree to hold harmless the Author from and against any damages, costs, and expenses, including any legal fees potentially resulting from the application of any of the information provided by this guide. This disclaimer applies to any damages or injury caused by the use and application, whether directly or indirectly, of any advice or information presented, whether for breach of contract, tort, negligence, personal injury, criminal intent, or under any other cause of action.

You agree to accept all risks of using the information presented inside this book. You need to consult a professional medical practitioner in order to ensure you are both able and healthy enough to participate in this program.

Table of contents

Introduction 1

Chapter 1: Timeline Of Ancient China - The Imperial Dynasties 3

Chapter 2: The Threat That Was Genghis Khan... 18

Chapter 3: Communism's Rise As Well As The Fall Of Communism 23

Chapter 4: China's Role On The Global Chessboard 31

Chapter 5: China's State Controlled Media 38

Chapter 6: Transforming Chinese Industries... 45

Chapter 7: History Of Chinese Language 53

Chapter 8: Introduction Traditional Chinese Medicine.. 62

Chapter 9: Chinese Religions And Culture 73

Chapter 10: Famous Tourist Attractions 83

Chapter 11: Chinese Traditional Folktales.. 90

Chapter 12: Story Of China As Well As United Kingdom Relationship 95

Chapter 13: Story Of Chinese Relationship With The Soviet And Russia 108

Chapter 14: On The Relationship Between China As Well As The United States 121

Chapter 15: Prehistory 141

Chapter 16: Ancient China 145

Chapter 17: Imperial China 154

Introduction

China is now among the most influential nations around the globe. The astonishing increase in their economy over the past few years has changed China from a place which was plagued by bloody civil wars to an edgy metropolis.

Are you curious to learn more about the Chinese's past? Are you interested in knowing how and why the once-stifling country suddenly opened its borders and allowed foreign influence in? This book you'll learn more about it.

This book will provide you with an overview of the history of China beginning with the different dynasties , emperors and emperors who had ruled the land and the rise of Genghis Khan and the turbulent time in which it was the Communist Party held the reins of the power. This book will also provide you an understanding of crucial questions such as the reason why China has blocked a significant portion web access. It will answer questions like what is the story behind how what happened to the Chinese medical and language get their start? What's the process by which the Chinese media function? What significance does China play in the global arena of political affairs today? What is the reason why China changed its strategy to create its own products instead of reproducing? Also, you will learn some of China's vibrant tradition, religions, as well as popular tourist destinations.

Chapter 1: Timeline of Ancient China - The Imperial Dynasties

Many Westerners are, unfortunately, influenced by misconceptions about China. Many think that China's long period of isolation has made China less strong and less successful as Western counterparts, but this is not the case. Sure, trade with the West ended abruptly during late in the Ming Dynasty, but this didn't significantly change China's influence over other nations in Asia This implies that it was an important economic driver in the region, either regardless of the assistance of Westerners. The Chinese economy was as strong as it is today regardless of trading agreements with the West The strength was due to their leaders.

In the past powerful and powerful families controlled China These were called the Dynasties. Much like the way the aristocracy operated throughout the West, Dynasties are ruled by the Emperor, who then passes it onto his nearest kin, usually the son with the highest rank. There was only one way to alter the family that was ruling was by creating a rebellion and then putting another clan in the throne.

In the last five thousand years, the control of China was in the hands of over 12 dynasties. And naturally, there were some that were more powerful than others were. This is a timeline of China's past at the beginning of time and ending in the present. We'll take a more in-depth review of some of China's most powerful and influential Dynasties to ever rule across Ancient China. We will also discuss how they got their the position of power and what they did to the entire society.

The Prehistoric Period (1.7 million years prior to the 21st Century BC)

The lengthy Prehistoric Times record the activities of the first humans during early Paleolithic Age, the maternal clan society during the first phase of the Neolithic Age, the transfer to paternal clan societies and Yangshao Culture during the middle of the period, and Longshan Culture as well as other human cultures in the latter part of the Neolithic Age. From 4,000 to 5 000 years ago, Chinese society was in the new century with increased production and, in particular, various handicrafts techniques.

Xia Dynasty (21st - 17th century BC)

In the beginning, as the only hereditary lineage in the ancient Chinese historical records, Xia was established by Qi, grandson of Yu the Great. It was a country of league that was a result of different tribes.

Shang Dynasty (17th - 11th century BC)

Shang was repeatedly ruled by 31 Emperors. It was founded by the Tang as the leader. Tang the Great, a society that was founded on slavery. It flourished during this dynasty, and left plenty of artifacts.

Western Zhou (11th century BC 771 BC)

Zhou Wuwang (Ji Fa) defeated Shang and established Western Zhou. The dynasty lasted for around 277 years. The dynasty created the first Han Chinese nationality by unifying minorities. The initial height of power and glory was attained in the feudal system of the ancient China.

The Autumn and Spring Season (770 BC - 476 BC)

This was the initial half of Eastern Zhou, in which more than a hundred schools of thought fought with Confucianism, among them. Many Vassal states, especially those that were ruled by the five main overlords, fought for the rule of the state.

Warring States Period (476 BC from 221 BC)

The time of division was amidst China as the title suggests. It was a time of continuous war between seven main Vassal States: Qi, Chu, Yan, Han, Zhao, Wei, and Qin.

Qin Dynasty (221 BC - Qin Dynasty (221 BC - BC)

The Emperor Qin Shi Huang Qin established China's first unification of feudal dynasties, Qin. The characters , weights and measurements became standardized for the very first time in China in the period. The tyranny of the time led to the fall of the dynasty, which just 15 years.

Western Han (206 BC - 24 AD)

The effective methods of Qin were adopted by Western Han. Western Han continued tax reduction policies that led to massive improvement in the fields of agriculture, handicrafts and trade, particularly under the reign of the The Emperors Wendi as well as Jingdi.

Xin Dynasty (8 - 23 AD)

The Xin Dynasty was founded by Wang Mang after rebelling against the Western Han.

Eastern Han (25 - 220 AD)

The Silk Road was made accessible to Europe in Eastern Han. Other significant changes include the introduction of Buddhism in China and the development of Taoism.

Three Kingdoms Period (220 - 220 - 280 AD)

The trilateral conflict among the three kingdoms Wei, Shu, and Wu is the most well-known aspect of this time.

Western Jin (265 - 316 AD)

Sima Yan established Western Jin. It ruled for 37 years. unbroken rule during that unstable period.

Eastern Jin (317 - 420 AD)

Eastern Jin was established by Sima Rui. It took Jiankang (Nanjing) for its capital, battling various small regimes in north.

Five Huns and Sixteen States (304 439 AD)

A variety of dividing regimes coexisted throughout the time. This led to an extremely turbulent one. Five Huns controlled the central plain, and sixteen states were ruled in the north.

Northern Dynasties (386 - 581 AD)

It refers to the regimes of North China then - North Wei, East Wei, West Wei, etc. which ended the 150 years of war.

Sui Dynasty (581 - 618 AD)

The most significant contribution made by the Sui Dynasty was the foundation of the Imperial Examination System.

Southern Dynasties (420 - 589 AD)

Song, Qi, Liang Chen Dynasties were throughout Southern China than to make the Southern Dynasties.

Tang Dynasty (618 - 907 AD)

Tang Dynasty is known as the most prosperous the dynasty in early Chinese history. The area was greatly expanded. Significant changes took place in the military, economy diplomacy, politics as well as the cultural, due to the shrewd administration of Emperors. Tang culture's influence Tang culture was not limited to China only, but neighbouring countries as well as the entire world was influenced by its influence.

Five Dynasties and Ten States (907 to 979 AD)

During this period of conflict five dynasties followed each other in the central plains, and 10 revolting regimes were born.

Northern Song (960 - 1127 AD)

North Song was founded by Zhao Kuangyin. It put an end the liberation that followed the Tang Dynasty.

Southern Song (1127 - 1279 AD)

Zhao Gou founded his own Southern Song, which was powerful in science, economics and technology, however lacking in military strategies and political strategies.

Liao Dynasty (916 - 1125 AD)

The feudal dynasty was created in the year 206 by Yelv Abaoji (the head of the Khitan clans) Liao. This dynasty controlled the northern part of China.

Western Xia Dynasty (1038 - 1227 AD)

In the beginning, it was named Da Xia, Western Xia was established in the year 2000 by Tanguts (Dongxiang) the people who govern the western region of China.

Jin Dynasty (1115 - 1234 AD)

North China was ruled during the time of Jin by the Jurchen people who established Jin.

Yuan Dynasty (1271 - 1368 AD)

It was the first unification system that was led by the first minorities throughout the entire time of China. It was established by Mongolians.

Ming Dynasty (1368 - 1644 AD)

Zhu Yuanzhang was the founder of the Ming Dynasty. The Ming Dynasty was the final feudal monarchy to be ruled by the Han people. The total of 19 emperors were ruled over 279 years.

Qing Dynasty (1644 - 1911 AD)

It was China's final feudal dynasty. It was founded by Manchu people. The country was transformed into semi-feudal, semi-colonial society in the last quarter of the dynasty.

Republic of China (1912 - 1949 AD)

The feudal system in place for more than two millennia ended , and China entered a time of war, reform as well as reconstruction and growth.

People's Republic of China (1949 to present)

With a growing strength of the nation and an unique oriental cultural heritage, China is the second largest economy.

Let's review some of the most significant family dynasties, in particular, their reigns and their influence.

The Han Dynasty

While not the longest-ruling dynasty (that distinction belongs to the Zhou dynasty, which was in power from 1046 BC until the year 256 BC) The four hundred years during which the Han Dynasty controlled China might be the most prosperous throughout the country's long history. Following when the Qin Dynasty had unified the kingdoms of China in the early years, they Han Dynasty kept them all togetherand set the precedent for the kinds of institutions the subsequent dynasties would use to ensure that the people were happy.

By using a more efficient method of taxation through a more efficient tax system, by a better taxation system Han Dynasty was able to keep its control over the political system and military strength far better than previous dynasties preceding it. Additionally to this, the Han obtained monopolies on salt and iron in the majority areas of the Asian region, resulting in an explosive expansion of their riches.

In order to increase its coffers due to its enormously growing coffers, the Han extended the boundaries of China in the past, moving it from its original core region within the Yellow River valley, to the present-day region called Southern China. The expansion was advantageous for China since the rice harvests in this region meant that China could sustain more people. Because of the wealth that the Han Dynasty gathered, China has become a major sociopolitical power in Asia that has made it much easier for it to take on and incorporate its kingdoms in the neighboring regions.

The creation of the Silk Road. Silk Road

Although it was true that the Han Dynasty was quite powerful however, it had to face a variety of problems such as the tribes of nomads from the north, called the Xiongnu which is also known as the Huns. These wandering raiders would attack Chinese travelers and merchants as a result of which the prior Qin Dynasty felt the need to construct the Great Wall. After they took over the Han Dynasty took over, instead of being focused in defense they aimed to take on the Huns and they had an army that was larger than prior to. These military operations brought about a variety of significant discovery within Central Asia. Central Asian region.

These military trips may have alerted China that there were other civilisations. They used to believe that they were the only state-run society on earth and that the rest of humanity was made up of barbarians, like the Xiongnu. At this time it was during this time that the Chinese discovered more about India and the Persians and the Bactrians as well as other ancient Asian civilizations. This knowledge was the basis for the establishment of trade routes that would improve China's socioeconomic standing and were later referred to in the Silk Road. To control this Silk Road, the Han controlled the majority of Xinjiang province and allowed the Chinese to expand their influence further into Western countries.

The Tang Dynasty

While the time that China was under the Han Dynasty ruled over China was among the most prosperous periods the China has ever known but it was still required to be ended somehow and did so after a bloody civil conflict was declared. After the demise of the Han Dynasty, the country was thrown into a few years of division and then split into smaller, autonomous regions till the Sui Dynasty took control and brought together China again. But after only 38 years (581 between 581 and 581 - 618 AD) and only three emperors Sui Dynasty ended, and the Tang Dynasty took its place.

In the Tang Dynasty, China opened its doors towards foreign influences making China more international than it had ever been. It was also thought of as the golden period in Imperial China.

In the Tang Dynasty rule, China expanded its territory to the northeast as well as in the south, they took over a significant portion of Manchuria and the entirety of Vietnam. In the course of this massive expansion that China began to influence the growth of state societies in neighboring states like the ones in Japan, Korea, and Tibet.

The Tang Dynasty's successes were due to their formidable army. The thing that made the military of the Tang so powerful was the adoption of the same combat styles as steppe nomads, who resulted in the cavalry. The first time that was the case, the Chinese army had its individual horses. They were uncommon in China. The Silk Road allowed the introduction from domesticated animal breeds into the Empire that included horses. The Chinese began cultivating their own horse, and then donating their horses to the army. they eliminated the main advantage that the nomadic tribes of northern Africa enjoyed.

The Tang Dynasty started to collapse when An Lushan, a general from Central Asia, incited a rebellion and declared himself Emperor. The subsequent fights, famines, and the spread of diseases nearly reduced the population by half in China which resulted in the An Lushan rebellion one of the biggest man-made disasters of the history of mankind. Because of the assistance from Tibet and Turkey and Turkey, the

Tang Dynasty barely defeated the rebels, but the empire was unable to hold its own since it was unable to recover from the destruction caused through the bloody civil conflict.

The Qing Dynasty

Following the demise of Tang Dynasty, several other Dynasties were in power over China. But none had the economic, political, or military will to sustain their reign. It was the Ming Dynasty, even though it was not afflicted by any serious threat, was one of the worst leaders within China. Chinese empire. The situation changed when the Qing Dynasty (1644-1911) held the power of the state. While it was the last Chinese Dynasty, it was also among its most powerful.

Chapter 2: The Threat that Was Genghis Khan

Prior to the building the Great Wall, the Chinese have always built walls and fortifications as attempt to dissuade intruders, especially those who were from the northern steppes which were the Mongols. In the past they were able to defend themselves enough, but once Temujin was the commander of the huge Mongol army and the Mongol army was going be changed for China but not necessarily in a positive way.

Temuzu's Rise Rise of Temujin

Temujin The man who would become named Genghis Khan, and who would later establish his own Mongol Empire, had less than humble beginnings. The fact that his life on the steppes was difficult can be described as an exaggeration. One of the earliest factors for Khan's dangerous upbring was that his mother was abducted by the tribe of his father and was forced into marriage. When Temujin's mom gave birth to the child, witnesses reported that there was the blood clot with his left hand. which was a signal of the baby's set to achieve greater heights. It was a tough time for Temujin, however his experiences led him to become one of one of the greatest leaders the people of the nomadic tribal tribes from Mongolia have ever seen.

Once he consolidated control over his family by killing his half-brother in law, Temujin began creating alliances with tribes of other nomadic tribes. This were easy due to his intimidating presence. Contrary to other leaders who were before him, he regarded merit to determine his promotion within his ranks. however, he did not let blood ties influence his decision-making. After a few years the Temujin army grew to a huge number of warriors. This comprised people from various religions. In 1205, he had defeated or defeated all the tribes of nomadic people in the steppes and brought their lands in his reign. The next year, he helped the leaders of the various tribes formed their own nation. they declared Temujin the Chinggis Khan which translates to "Universal Ruler" or, as people of the west refer to him as Genghis Khan.

Many people are unaware that Genghis Khan wasn't a savage. Genghis Khan was actually a civilized and well-off man. In his time in order to end intertribal conflict He threw out the aristocratic titles , and let the people pick their own leaders. He also prohibited the kidnapping and the selling of tribal women, prohibited the slavery of other Mongols and made theft of livestock the crime that could be punished with death. Genghis Khan also introduced the nation-wide adoption of a written system, permitted the freedom of religion and conducted a regular count of his own domain. The Mongols were actually practicing a primitive kind of democracy if the way you look at this, but it was more favourable than the current dynasty was using.

It was the Conquest of the Jin Dynasty

Within a year of ascending to the throne, Genghis Khan launched what would be a series of fights designed to take control over the Western Xia territory. This is important as the territory it was located along the Yellow River was one of the biggest garrisons of the Chinese Empire. After a few years and numerous bloody battles after, Western Xia fell to the Mongol Empire. This signaled the beginning of the rapid expansion in Mongols. Mongols as well as the expanding of their territories.

One of the most important objectives for Genghis Khan was topple his father, the Jin Dynasty of China, mostly to bring revenge on another Mongol Khan and get access to the wealth in Northern China, and to consolidate their status as a superpower in East Asia. Genghis Khan also wanted to establish a strong position as a superpower. Jin Emperor also committed the mistake of asking the surrender by Mongol troops to Chinese rule. Mongol Army for Chinese rule.

While Genghis Khan and his Mongol group had no issues in taking on China's Chinese troops on the field, Genghis Khan had trouble in destroying the city's fortifications. With the assistance by Chinese engineers who sided with his side and his Mongols were able develop siege weapons that enabled them to take control of the most fortified cities.

After securing several defenses Genghis Khan believed that it was high time He wiped out his enemies, the Jin Dynasty for good. The year 1213 was the time. He took his troops deep to the territory of the enemy, which was situated between the Yellow River and the Great Wall. After two years with the aid of a high Jin officer who joined the Mongols Genghis Khan took over and seized the capital of the Dynasty, Yanjing (Beijing), making it necessary for the Emperor Xuanzong to relocate the capital of the empire to Kaifeng.

Chapter 3: Communism's Rise as well as the Fall of Communism

In World War II, an uncertain alliance developed between china's ruling Nationalist Party (the Kuomintang) and the Communist Party led by Chairman Mao Zedong. After the conflict, China was almost in destruction and in serious financial difficulties, all of which led to that the war that existed between Kuomintang and the Communist Party. Kuomintang as well as the Communist Party finally dissolved and led to a bloody civil war to gain control of China. In 1949 the Communists were able to force the Kuomintang to withdraw, which reduced to the Chinese Republic's (ROC) areas to Taiwan in addition to Hainan (the later to be relegated in later Communist control). On the 10th of October that year the Mao Zedong was elected Chairman. Mao Zedong proclaimed the rise of the People's Republic of China, plunged the entire country into communism.

It's the Great Leap Forward

Chairman Mao visited the Chinese countryside and concluded that the Chinese could achieve anything if they unify around the same goals. He believed that if people focused their efforts on industries as well as agriculture, the economy would increase and even surpass America. United States in just a couple of years. In 1958 the Chairman Mao declared the start of a five-year strategy to transform China into a major economic force and he dubbed this strategy"The Great Leap Forward.

Mao believed that industry and agriculture, working together would aid both develop. The fields would make sure that the workers in industry were fed and the industry would supply the most modern equipment and equipment that help to make farming more efficient. To make his dream be realized, Mao needed everyone in China to be in agreement with his vision, and which is why he took his people and put them in a set of communal homes, the majority of which were home to approximately 55,000 families.

The citizens would surrender everything they own in the community, and the commune ensures that they receive everything they require to live comfortably. The commune would provide everything citizens would require, including entertainment. This meant that people were no longer making money for themselves They would do in the interest of the entire community.

In the year 1958, nearly 700 million people had been shifted into 30,000 communal areas across the nation. Despite the fact that it involved removing individuals from their ancestral homes and taking their possessions away Incessant propaganda from the government managed to inspire enthusiasm among the people. Every person in the commune was not just expected to meet production quotas, but it was "urged" to beat them.

The Great Leap Forward encouraged each commune to set up their own production facilities which comprised more than half one million backyard smelts which made steel for all communes. In the period when all of these smelts had been in operation, they made eleven million tons of iron each year, a record amount.

The demise of the five-year plan

In its initial year, The Great Leap Forward showed tremendous potential, but the situation quickly changed in the next year. The party officials that ruled the communes, who were determined to be better than each other and make outrageous demands of the population as they increased their production limits and demanded that them focus on the manufacturing of machinery and steel rather than farming. In the absence of enough food for the workers and the industrial component of the communes began to slow. It was also not helping that the cheap and substandard farming equipment given to farmers often broke down and not contribute significantly to the agricultural sector.

The situation became so dire that China faced a huge food shortage, which forced the government to limit food items to people living in communes. Many people perished due to the famine which resulted from Mao's Five-year Plan failing which significantly impacted Mao's power and popularity with the Chinese people. This was the reason he decided to go ahead with his second major strategy in 1966. which was the Cultural Revolution.

The Cultural Revolution

Chairman Mao's Great Proletarian Cultural Revolution took the place in 1966 and lasted until 1976. It sought to protect the core concept of Communism by removing the remnants of capitalism and the old elements of Chinese society and culture. Cultural Revolution Cultural Revolution wanted to impose "Maoist" views as the primary political philosophy within the Communist Party.

Mao blamed capitalists as well as "revisionists" for the entirety of what failed in the Great Leap Forward. Therefore, when Mao declared the start of the Cultural Revolution, he wanted to destroy any ideology that didn't align in his view. At the time that the government was in power, they employed an array of tactics to denigrate the bourgeoisie and convince the masses that Mao's plans are beneficial to the nation. The campaign was on the magnitude of they actually convinced people they Mao was not an ordinary mortal; He was actually sent by God to guide China on the right track.

Mao's Red Guards scoured the countryside to burn everything that was that was related to traditional Chinese culture, books, and other documents that originated from the West They even detained and often executed teachers who didn't share the same beliefs like members of the Communist Party. Anyone who opposed Mao or his leadership Mao or his doctrines were targeted for punishment, even if they didn't intend to make a statement that was negative in the event that Mao's Red Guard deemed they were in error, they were imprisoned and was beaten. In reality, the Cultural Revolution was actually more like a purge with the intention to clean the new slate to ensure that China could begin afresh. In the ten years that China was under the grip of the Cultural Revolution was in effect numerous scholars and educators were detained and then executed.

While the Chairman Mao Zedong himself said that the Cultural Revolution ended in 1969 but their purging actions and mass media were operating up to the time of his death in the year 1976. Mao's successor Hua Guongfeng claimed that Mao Zedong at his funeral wrotein his deathbed "With you as my boss I'm comfortable," supposedly to get the people to join his reign. However, the public as well as the rest of the Party already knew Hua for his sluggish in terms of political ability and ambition than the Chairman before him He was also unable to gain the trust of the people, or even the complete trust of the Communist Party. A month after his death as Chairman Mao the bloodless coup overthrew and re-established the Communist Party, and Deng Xiaoping was elected chairman of the People's Republic of China.

The surge of capitalism

After the death of Chairman Mao Zedong and the fall of the Communist Party, the reformists under the leadership of Deng Xiaoping, started to introduce reforms to the economic system of China. They sought to reverse the harm caused through Mao's failed Five-year plan along with the Cultural Revolution. The Chairman Deng Xiaoping started by signing an historic accord in 1979 with the then US president Jimmy Carter, effectively ending years of tensions between the two countries and opening China's frontiers for foreign investment.

Deng Xiaoping enacted some economic reforms, a majority of which restored the right of the citizens to manage their own business. The Chairman also created and created four major economic zones on the southern coast of China in an effort to lure foreign investors into China. In a single breath, China transformed from a country that hated capitalism to one that embraced capitalism. China went through a transition from communes into an economic system in which it is legal to own property, and people can retain the earnings from their own enterprises and the government is embracing the idea of competition in the free market.

Chapter 4: China's role on the Global Chessboard

China officially passed Japan in February 2011 and become the world's second largest economy. The pace of growth has was a little slower because of the crisis in debt in the Eurozone in the early months of 2012. China continues to grow and is improving its economy each year. As a member of the World Trade Organization, China is able to access markets outside of its own which it is able to reap. Trading partners have expressed concern about the fact that China should boost its value for Renminbi (Chinese money) to ensure that its products are more expensive to foreign buyers and exports will be delayed. China has been forced to resort to gradual relaxation of the restrictions on trading with the currency.

The need for energy is rising in China due to its rapid growth economy. China is the world's largest oil producer and consumer and the second biggest oil user after the USA. Billions of dollars are splurged by China in pursuit of foreign energy sources.

The change in the political landscape in China is not as rapid as the economic transformation and as the Communist Party (world's largest political party) remains in authority and holds a tight grip over the people. Dissidents who speak out are sent to labour camps, and the authorities are able to repress any indication of discontent.

The President of the moment Xi Jinping rose to power in 2012-13 and was a hand-picked successor to Hu Jintao; he is likely to be the leader of China over the coming 10 years. A radical shift away from the old political system is anticipated under Xi because he has placed more the power of his hand (a shift away from collective governance). Xi has been focusing on economic reforms to improve market forces, and an the fight against corruption that has increased his popularity. The Western concepts of human rights and democracy to serve as examples for China are not popular with Xi and his party. has censored opinions, which is not in accordance with the system of one-party rule, particularly in social media.

China is a member of numerous international organisations and has an important role in many of them, including permanent membership in the United Nations' Security Council. China is a signatory to the Non-Proliferation Treaty in the UN context as nuclear power. China's foreign policy China is currently summed in terms of a strategic policy for its neighbours as well as superpowers around the world, to pursue China's national interests (the interests that is the interest of China's Communist Party as well) as well as bringing its growth to a point where China can be competitive with other countries in the long time.

The formal relationship with the U.S. were established in 1979. Though both nations are in agreement on international issues, such as climate change and terrorism However, they have had to endure tense relations in the past 25 years regarding contentious issues such as trade balance, Taiwan, nuclear proliferation and intellectual property rights and human rights.

Chinese leaders have been travelling across the globe over the past few times and China has risen to a higher image within the UN due to its constant presence at the Security Council and other international organisations.

China's Influence on Asia

Although China's growing role in Asia may not have been well-received by Westerners, China has worked towards ensuring the security of its continent specifically the Korean Peninsula. China has also developed relations of cooperation with countries of ASEAN (Association of Southeast Asian Nations). Territorial disputes within the South China Sea have remained mostly unresolved, despite the constant efforts of the UN. These disputes concern the maritime claims as well as the islands. China is involved in most of the dispute. other sovereign nations are Brunei, Taiwan, Malaysia, Philippines, and Vietnam. These disputes can have the Chinese with a bad image internationally.

To serve as a counterbalance to strength of United States, the relationship between China and Russia has been reformed dramatically. Treaty of Friendship and Cooperation was signed in the year 2001. The two countries also joined Shanghai Cooperation Organization (SCO) which helps to ensure stability in the region.

Two of the largest nations around the globe and the relations with China and India was never this peaceful. Both countries had weaker ties all through the twentieth century. The first talks took place for first time since 2003 following the Sino-Indian War of 1962 (the dispute about Aksai Chin as well as South Tibet has still not been resolved, despite). Both states began collaborating in economic and strategic areas as well, and China was the most important commercial partner to India in the year 2010. India opposes Chinese military assistance towards its archrival Pakistan as well as its neighbours Bangladesh as well as Bangladesh. China opposes the growing military collaboration between India and Japan and China, the United States, and Australia.

China's displeasure with the proposal to provide permanent seats to 2 of its neighbours which include India and Japan is considered to be cause for anger within their respective relations. Japan is the strongest adversary and ally of China due to its vast cultural and economic influence throughout Asia.

All 193 UN members are recognized by China However, 22 sovereign states don't accept that the People's Republic of China as the sole legally valid Chinese state. Vatican City is among these nationsthat use the term "Republic of China" to refer to China as the Republic of China (Taiwan) but doesn't recognize the People's Republic of China.

Changes in China's Global Policies and Role

China is focused on enhancing its relations to Russia and Europe in order to counterbalance China's influence on the United States in the late 1990s and into the 20th century. The goal was to maintain a check over U.S. power through alliances with other powers. Following an intervention by the U.S. intervention in Kosovo the assessment was rethought and China defined its foreign policy within an unipolar global. This led to China's security concept being reformulated, which suggested that countries should be thinking in terms of the economic and diplomatic co-operation instead of thinking in terms of alliances or power blocs.

China is running a number of initiatives to build an image of its Communist Party overseas. The emphasis of Xi on openness in the local level of government decision-making at the sixth Plenum of 2016 was just one of numerous examples.

China's influence in the world's politics has increased since the beginning of its existence. The post-cold-war era has seen China's economy rise to new levels. "With wealth goes power" is just as relevant in the present as it was back when U.S. rose to power as well, and China is set to be a key player in the shaping for the next century.

Chapter 5: China's State Controlled Media

China has the largest global media marketplace and the biggest online population of all countries also belongs to China. The communist party holds complete control over media outlets. The media industry is restricted to distribution, publishing and advertising, however, there is no space to edit content. Independent coverage is permitted to those outlets that aren't considered to be an affront to the political system or to the stability of the nation overall.

Based on Reporters Without Borders (RSF), China is the world's most infamous prison for journalists and online dissidents. The report issued by the organisation (World Press Freedom Index) declares it is the case that China's Communist Party has reached a new level of repression in which "Journalists were not spared including abductions, forced confessions on television and threats to family members."

Rebroadcasting of foreign news is strictly prohibited. Satellite receivers blocks shortwave broadcasts and block websites.

News outlets in Chinese that are not controlled or controlled by the government are restricted within mainland China. International English websites in the English language are generally available, however content that isn't compatible with the China's Communist Party's policies is blocked. In times of tension there are many English news sites in the English language are blocked.

The television industry is highly extremely competitive, with virtually every person having a television within their homes (especially in the cities). The amount of local, regional as well as national television channels are greater than 3300. Chinese Central TV or the CCTV is the most powerful state-owned media corporation. The provincial TVs compete with its supremacy by airing national programs through satellite. Pay TV is a significant marketplace in China. The number of radio stations is more than 2,600 operating in China which are all owned by the government.

The total amount of newspapers in circulation is approximately 1900. Each locality has its own name that is published by the local authority, and there is an official regional Communist Party daily as well.

China is spending huge sums on radio, TV online, and other media outline that are targeted at international viewers. The intention is to increase the influence of China's political leaders and improve general Chinese image. Foreign companies are not welcomed in China's market.

China's Online Growth

China is home to the world's largest internet-connected population, with 668 million internet users (China Internet Network Information Center CNNIC). According to CNNIC 89% of people who are online have access to the internet through a smartphones.

The market for online products is controlled by 3 giants. Baidu is the leading search engine; gaming online is controlled by Tencent the top microblog platform. Weibo is managed by the e-commerce kingpin Alibaba along with Sina. Weibo is losing its popularity as a place where free-of-censorship news can be posted due to the government-imposed suppression.

WeChat is the alternative to WhatsApp instant messaging was home to more than 700 million active users at the end of the year, making it the most well-known social network in China.

The video streaming platforms such as Alibaba's Youku Tudou and Sohu are challenging to traditional TVs , with a growing number of subscribers.

"Great Chinese Firewall" is a comprehensive web filtering and blocking system that blocks an array of websites by using URL screening and keyword censoring. Advanced and modern technology is employed by China to regulate and monitor the online content that users access. Cyber police watch on the internet and content classified as politically sensitive or socially sensitive is restricted. Twitter, Facebook, Youtube as well as a handful of human rights websites are among the sites that are blocked. The tools for circumventing the block have become increasingly difficult in the past few times. The firewall has been bolstered by China to snoop on data traffic from and to specific IP addresses. It was known as"the "Great Fire Cannon" when it was first operational in the year 2015.

Here are some crucial printing presses:

* Renmin Ribao (People's Daily) is a Communist Party daily, web pages in English

* Global Times Global Times English pages on languages, run by the state and focusing on global events

* Cankao Xiaoxi (Reference News) It is released through the agency for news Xinhua

Radio:

* China National Radio - State-run

* China Radio International - external broadcaster owned by the state.

Programs that span more than forty languages. It also broadcasts to Taiwan as well as Korea as well

Official TV channel is Chinese Central TV (CCTV) that is a nation-wide state-owned broadcaster. It is comprised of the CCTV network, which is also known as the English news channel.
News. Xinhua is an official news agency of the state with webpages in English.

A Note on Freedom of Expression

Freedom of speech is a right and not an entitlement in China. Free Speech Elite is a term that refers to individuals who are able to voice their opinions and even criticize the government (not entirely, however). These are people who were a members of the Communist Party or senior member of the government. The only people who are able to effectively voice their grievances are the senior participants of the Communist Party, this group is known as"the ideological elite. The second group is the professional and intellectual elite that includes editors and academics of government-controlled publications. They have some freedom (although not as much as

Communist Party officials) which implies that they are able to challenge the policies of the government. The boundaries of this group is determined by the people they're able to reach. For instance the government would not be averse to criticizing if it's done in private conversations and academic conferences that are closed to the public or any other platform in which the government believes there's no risk of participation by the public.

The proportion of people belonging to the various groups mentioned above is insignificant when you consider the total people in China. The billion or more citizens of China can voice their opinions of discontent privately however they aren't able to express their opinions in public. The average Chinese citizen's freedom to publish is actually referred to as the right to self-submit.

Chapter 6: Transforming Chinese Industries

China attracted the attention of the world and grew exponentially in the field of industrial. China was famous for contract manufacturing OEMs (Original Equipment Manufacturers) as well as the entire product range was stuffed with cheap electronic products, no-name brands as well as textiles and other products from different sectors. China did not compete for high quality of its products, but instead focused on the quantity of goods and trying to produce products at a lower cost that they were able to. But this is not the case anymore as China becoming more quality-oriented. The companies have moved to new designs, brand identities and distinctive products. This change is rapid and a large number of producers are now making this radical transformation. There are many reasons this transformation occurred.

The majority of the companies started with a small scale, and the products they produced were enough for the brands they worked for. The brands were not developed therefore they had to make to produce the product at a lower cost because of the very competitive market. This meant there was no distinction between most small-scale manufacturers as all of the brands had the same name, but they all produced the same product. Through the years, small-scale manufacturers that remained in business expanded by working for multiple businesses. This increased their size and provided them with the ability to think about more than just creating products. This resulted in a shift where the pursuit of quality was more important than quantity.

Gaoyu Electronics is a factory located in the Laokeng Industrial Zone of Pingshan located situated in Shenzhen. It is a small company that produces cooling technology that are used in electronic equipment. This company is an excellent illustration of the change which many other businesses are experiencing. The company is similar to other companies in Shenzen's Industrial belt.

The company began 15 years ago, making DC fan and heatsinks, which were then re-assembled to make cooling fans. They were manufactured by

Huaqiangbei (the company that Gaoyu Electronic worked on contract). Gaoyu Electronics grew over the years and was awarded contracts by other companies such as Cisco as well as Foxconn. The company's growth has convinced its owners to consider a different approach to producing goods for different companies as well. Gaoyu Electronics launched its own brand name, Ecotherm in 2014.

Ecotherm is a brand utilized in Gaoyu Electronics to produce innovative products that incorporate smart technology. Companies such as Gaoyu Electronics are hiring a number of engineers in the department of research and development.

Over the past couple of decades, producers from all sectors have increased their earnings potential and the complexity of their operations. The majority of these producers began by contracting or working as OEMs. They made already-designed products or even parts of products for other businesses. As technology improved production, many companies moved to the concept of original design manufacturers (ODM). Instead of simply replicating the designs, producers began handling the design process, and creating innovative products of their own which other businesses would mark their name on prior to selling it at retail.

The changes occurred in nearly every industry, however one of the main factors that quickly altered the situation is it was the European crisis. In the aftermath of this, demand for Chinese products dropped across the world and the companies were left with a surplus of inventory that were not sold. One option was to write their names on the product, and then remove them from markets in the area.

This was only the start of a trend that will eventually bring China toward a new objective. In factories across China which were attracted to copying products and then make them look like that original item (from an innovative brand) moved to the development of brands. The reasoning is straightforward that the profit margins for OEMs were being squeezed by more companies producing the same product, but the demand for it was slowing globally. The traditional OEMs were influenced by companies such as Xiaomi and Haier which have higher profits, but not getting whipped as OEMs.

This strategy was successful It not only helped the current OEMs to survive during a critical moment but also created the business model that could follow by newcomers for success at home as well as abroad. The margin for profit of self-branded products is 10 times greater than the product that is sold through an intermediary within the United States for a factory located in China. The brand is a profitable alternative to conventional Chinese OEMs.

The central government of China plays a significant part in this change. It is encouraging companies to create new designs and then developing with their own labels. The approach employed is straightforward high-level officials are in factories, speaking about the importance of innovation during public addresses and implementing preferential economic policies for local businesses and reorienting people away from foreign brands across the country. The government also offers significant funding programs to initiatives that promote innovations. The brands that are backed by the government receive massive incentives. The aim is to establish China Inc. brand worldwide and create high-value jobs.

The government's efforts have proven to be largely successful, since the consumer's mood has undergone an upswing in China. The term "Made from China" is no longer a reference to cheap, boring, and inferior items. The new Chinese brand names haven't just kept pace with their more developed foreign counterparts and have even outperformed them both in China and internationally.

A Case Study of Fashion Industry and Smartphones Smartphone and Fashion Industry Example

70% of smartphones sold in China were attributed to three foreign brand names: Samsung, Nokia, and Apple in the year 2011. There was a plethora of local electronic makers, and even though the local companies had begun to develop but they were viewed as cheap imitations that could not compete with the brands from abroad that were trusted. The general perception of the time was that most of people didn't want choose an indigenous brand.

Things have changed since then and just five years later Eight of the top ten brands in smartphones were locally-owned. Huawei along with Xiaomi were at the top spot after taking over foreign brands like Apple as well as Samsung. The trend continues through the year 2016. An indigenous Chinese media (hi-tech) company, Oppo has propelled past Apple and is now the second-most popular mobile brand China with a 67% increase over the previous year.

A stroll through any cell phone market in China will reveal a new trend where companies (like Laimi, Skyhan, Umi) are promoting their latest feature phones, hoping to be an alternative to Huawei.

Numerous reports from across the world suggest that seven of the 10 top smartphone brands around all over the globe are Chinese. Huawei isn't just the top smartphone manufacturer in China but it's also listed as the second-best smartphone in Europe and ranked as third in the world.

Like electronics clothing industry China is also experiencing this shift, as well as in the official policy and the consumer's perception.

The factories grew quickly and made millions using the designs of other countries. The factories copied the designs and then sold the designs at a lower cost. After that, there was a shift that prompted factories to create the production of their own.

The local government as well as the local community members echoed the same opinions. There aren't any rules or regulations that oblige factories to create their own brands, however the industry is pushing and the influence of government is typically very strong.

Many small-scale producers are following the path taken by Gaoyu Electronics. The inspiration comes coming from Huawei; Lenovo has become the top laptop manufacturer as well as Haier has established a respectable brand name in the appliance manufacturing.

Chapter 7: History of Chinese Language

It is believed that the Chinese written system of writing is the only one of a unique in its. It's unique in that it isn't based on the standard alphabetic scripts that are used in many other languages. This is a unique phenomenon that has developed over time, thanks to the use of characters and complicated signs that are a representation of phrases and words. While there are various languages which employ pictures or characters that are part of writing (Logography), Chinese is the only one to serve as the primary language for million of individuals.

Japanese or Korean written systems can be akin to Chinese system of writing, however they function as phonetic scripts. Although the first known Chinese writing system is believed to be around 3500 years old, its roots stretch further back in time. While putting the debate about its origins to one side, Chinese language has evolved through time, while maintaining its roots from the time of ancient times. This means that Chinese has been in use throughout the history of mankind for some of the longest periods of time anywhere in the world.

Origin and Evolution

The general consensus of historians is that the Chinese writing system developed from the non-linguistic symbols. In the second half of the 3rd millennium BCE (Late Neolithic period) Pictograms or symbols were carved on jades and pottery; These are believed to be the family symbols belonging to a particular civilization or dynasty that confirmed their ownership. A few of these emblems were used to identify the name of a Dynasty artifacts. There is a belief that, at some point, the symbols stopped being a representation of the image on them and became words. It is not clear when the switch occurred and yet it is generally accepted that the words we currently use today evolved from the symbol language. The possibility exists that symbols could be utilized as words at this time, but there isn't any proof to support such a claim.

Even though the first phase was in the middle, Chinese language had gathered many symbols, and was becoming quite complex in the Shang dynasty. Oracle bones scripts are the earliest version of Chinese writing that was used between 1500 to 1000 BCE. After etching the characters on turtle shells and animal bones it was then allowed to heat and interpreters were created when cracks appeared. The evidence is found in places where the system was utilized in courts.

Some of the complexities

One of the most common features in the writing process earlier is the use of'rebus writing.' Rebus writing means to utilize a symbol that represents an expression for another word that has a similar sound, but with a different meaning. A sample of English can help clarify the meaning. The symbol "4" actually refers to four, however it's used to symbolize the word 'for.' Chinese is monosyllabic languages, which implies the rebus script was employed extensively.

The most complicated aspect of that early Chinese script consisted of using the same symbol to signify two words that have somewhat similar meanings, yet totally different sounding (polysemy). For instance the sign that was used to represent two words "eye" (*muk) as well as "to observe" (*kens) were the identical. If all similar signs were used to signify different words, it could create confusion. To avoid this confusion the scribes began to add an additional symbol in order to differentiate between the signs. This resulted in the development in the form of compounds. The additional symbols are used to distinguish between the unclear words and to provide an equivalent meaning that could serve as a reference for other words too. This is why they are given the term "semantic determinatives" in which the new compound symbols are represented as part of a formula that can be used to make new words. In the contemporary Chinese language, they are known as "radicals," and they have been standard over the course of the course of.

Stages

The development of Chinese writing continued through the course of time. Following its initial development during the Shang Dynasty, the language was not static, but continued to evolve. In terms of the visual aspect, the language were more stylized, linear and began to resemble natural objects. The complexity was increased by the introduction of new radicals, which created new words.

It is believed that the Chinese writing system is divided into several scripts by experts. The initial four stages lasted for about 1500 years and major changes was observed during this time. Chinese evolved from a new written system that was unclear and pictographic to an improved standardization that included thousands of characters that continue to be used.

Oracle Bone Script (Jiaguwen in Chinese) was the first stage of Chinese writing, which was employed during the last period of the Shang Dynasty from 1500 - 1000 BCE. The next stage of writing was Greater Seal (Dazhuan) in which bronze vessels were utilized instead of bones to write. While the pictographic characters were slightly similar, their visual appearance changed because of the changes on the surfaces. Timelines of Oracle Bone Script and Greater Seal overlap, however they are thought to be distinct levels because the surface used for writing was distinct. Greater Seal is said to have been used from Late Shang to Western Chou dynasties (1100 - 700 BCE).

Lesser Seal (Xiaozhuan) was the next stage and is considered to be as the direct ancestor of the modern Chinese language. It was a transition towards an edgier representation of words. The use of radicals grew during this time, and is still being utilized in contemporary Chinese. Lesser Seal scripts are still being used to calligraphe in China.

The Clerkly Script (Lishu) It was utilized by bureaucrats in the government according to the name. The origin of the script dates back to around 500 BCE It was extensively utilized in the Qin and Han dynasties (221 between 206 and 221 BCE) by officials who required a fast and quick method of handling issues that governed the government. The primary distinction among Lishu the Lesser Seal and Lishu Lesser Seal is that the one has fewer strokes, and has a more fluid style to it. This implies the Lishu is more flexible, and is being used in this modern time at times.

These characters have been standardized to eliminate regional differences. The form that characterizes Lishu characters is identical to contemporary Chinese characters. It could be said it was Lishu was a stage of maturity in Chinese development of the language, and continued to be used until the 20th century.

The only distinct difference in the scripts that evolved following Lishu was that they became more cursive and were mostly used for calligraphy. The scripts that were developed comprise Standard Script (Kaishu), Running Script (Xingshu), and Grass Script (Caoshu).

A significant shift within the Chinese language took place during the time that China People's Republic of China (PRC) introduced an edgier form of Standard Script (Kaishu) in 1949. A lot of characters could not be further simplified, so it was only the characters were simplified that allowed them to be further simplified. The simpler version of the character (jiantizi) variant (Modern Chinese) was widely accepted by Singapore and other countries with Chinese as spoken, such as Hong Kong,

Taiwan, Chinese communities across the Americas as well as Southeast Asia declined this change and continued to use tradition (Kaishu). The simplified version did not gain more acceptance since it was political in nature and the roots of tradition are deep within Chinese cultural practices.

Influence

Chinese became an important basis for inspiration to writing systems from other parts of East Asia as it was one of the first and the sole indigenous writing systems in this region of Asia. Certain among these systems of writing remain in use , while others have gone extinct or have been merged with other writing systems. These scripts are described as"the "Sinitic group of scripts."

Two important scripts within that of the Sinitic Family include Japanese and Korean scripts.

In the beginning they Japanese wrote entirely in Chinese but they also developed their own language, grammar and syntax by using their Chinese language. This led to the creation of the three different scripts (kanji, hiragana and the katakana) that are currently being used. There is a possibility that each of three scripts can be used within the text.

Chinese script was modified to match the Korean language. This led to the development of Hanja script, which was later used to represent sound and words. The system was in use for over a thousand years before the introduction of the Hangul alphabet which is used today in North as well as South Korea.

Chapter 8: Introduction Traditional Chinese Medicine

The traditional Chinese treatment (TCM) is among the oldest medical systems. The background of Chinese medicine goes in the second century BC. It may have begun prior to that, but there is no basis to justify this idea. While there were written descriptions concerning the disease in the Shang Dynasty, nothing was discovered regarding the medical methods employed to treat the ailments. "Huangdi Neijing" often referred to by"the Yellow Emperor's Inner Canon was the first ever medical treatise to document the methods of medicine used in traditional Chinese medical practices. The techniques of acupuncture as well as Moxibustion were detailed and are still used today. Other treatises covered the various methods that were based on conventional physical concepts.

What exactly do these terms mean? What are the basic components in traditional Chinese medicine? In essence, Chinese medicine is based on the Daoist philosophy of harmony and considers all things in the universe as interconnected. The Chinese have created a unique method for understanding the function and structure in the human body and have referred to it The Traditional Chinese Medicine. Chinese medicine is based on eating and exercising to improve and sustain the health of the human race. If an illness or disease occurs, it is treated using herbs, acupuncture or moxibustion as well as Qigong. TCM is acknowledged as a reliable form of medicine throughout the world and practitioners are able to diagnose and treat various kinds of disease and illness. But, mastering and learning Chinese medicine is a complicated procedure.

TCM practitioners are of the view that mind and body create an energetic system that cannot be separated from one or from the entire universe. The same is true for the organs of the body that aren't separated, but they are connected and collaborate to ensure the normal function in the human body. TCM practitioners belief is in treating the person not the condition.

The main principle that is the basis of Chinese health can be described as Yin and Yang. Everything within the Universe are either Yin or Yang. However, there is no way to be completely Yin and all Yang Yet, a harmonious relationship between the two continues to evolve. Both are opposing energiesbut they are also similar. They're not independent of one another, but they do change to become one. For example it is the case that the day (Yang) changes into night (Yin) as winter (Yin) changes to the spring (Yang.) The cause of illness is excessive Yin or Yang that is present in the body. Treatment of diseases in the Chinese medical system is the practice of balancing the Yin and Yang that can be accomplished through acupuncture or herbs or Qigong. In contrast essential substances interact with each with each other to provide nourishment and support to the body. The most vital substances include Qi Blood, Qi and Fluids of the body, Fluids, Jing, and Shen. These essential substances are combined to create the brain and the body.

Qi The body is an energetic force (also called the vital force or the life force) and Qi flows through it. Qi circulates through the body through meridians or channels. Qi is a form of substance or energy. It is believed that the Chinese consider that "The physical body is created by Qi builds up and the body is destroyed as Qi is gone." Qi is responsible for the security as well as the maintenance of processes and systems of the body. the other vital elements are indications of Qi. Health is affected by the flow of Qi throughout the body. In the event that the flow of Qi through channels (pathways which connect all the organs) is disturbed, deficient or stagnant, there is a imbalance of Yin as well as Yang is disrupted, which could cause the illness.

Blood: Blood is of alternative significance in Chinese medicine as opposed to Western medicine. TCM practitioners believe that blood isn't only limited to providing nutrients, but also gives vitality in the body. Blood is a version of Qi. Zang Fu organs are the source of Qi. Zang Fu organs make blood through nourishment and drinks. Blood is essential for maturing our skin and muscles, as along with bones and organs. A stagnant or deficient blood supply could be the reason for ailment and occasionally, the heat of the blood can cause discomfort.

The Body Fluids: Jin Ye or Bodily Fluids are made up of nutrients. They work to fill with lubrication, nourish, and protect the body. Jin fluids include liquids to help lubricate the muscles, skin and the outside part of your body (sweat tears). Ye liquids, in contrast to the watery, light nature of Jin liquid are thick and heavy liquids that are lubricating joints, the mind, as well as inside the body. The problem may be caused due to deficient fluids in the body or the accumulation of excess body fluids.

Jing: Jing is the vital force through which Qi circulates. It is the source of energy and well-being for the human body. A strong Jing signifies that the body's makeup is strong. Conversely, a weak Jing signifies that the body's makeup is weak, which can make the body more prone to fall ill. Jing is the base of reproduction and life. In addition, it is in charge of the development and growth of our body. Problems with the constitution or development may lead to illness.

Shen: Shen is mind or spirit.

TCM as well as Western Medicine

The Qing Empire, especially in the 19th century, witnessed the surge of Western treatments in China. A large number of missionary doctors as well as Western practitioners travelled to the Qing Empire in addition, Western medical treatises started to appear. The revolutionaries and leaders following the Qing Dynasty wanted to implement and revive the traditional Chinese medical practices, however the doctor Dr. San Yet-sen , the founder of Western medicine was a most ardent advocate of Western medical practices and advocated for the practice and implementation of Western medical practices. He himself was a Western-trained doctor who played a pivotal part in the modernization of politics. Lateron, the communist party also sought to apply traditional medical practices in China. Through the Cultural Revolution, many practices were prohibited, and practitioners were also slandered.

In the present in China the cooperation among TCM with Western medicine has been in place for a long time especially in the field of ethnomedicine. But, there are a wealth of Chinese herbal substances which are still to be utilized for Western medicine. These substances and the theories that go in Chinese medical practices are of immense importance to Western medicine professionals and TCM practitioners too. Presently, TCM practitioners are interested in experimental and statistical methods to test the efficacy of the medicines. The majority of TCM hospital in China have electron microscopes. They use them for various lab tests.

In the West there are many medical schools that offer courses in alternative medicine into their curriculum. However, many older Western medical doctors and scientists regarded TCM as a pseudoscience and superstition. The differences in opinion be due to a variety of causes. TCM practice in Western countries is supported by Chinese immigrants, or people who have lost faith in conventional therapies. The application of Chinese medicine is also hampered due to cultural differences. For instance, a patient who has a fractured tooth in the West is unlikely to visit the Chinese practitioner or martial arts training school to get the bone fixed in a correct place. In fact it's a common issue in China.

It doesn't mean that TCM methods aren't considered important to those in the West. Indeed, a lot of Western drug companies have been undertaking studies on traditional medicine. In the end, many active pharmaceutical components that are used in Western medicines were actually extracted from animal and plant sources. In the case of Western medicines are involved, the ingredient must pass through the scientific tests in order to establish its effectiveness and efficacy. Thus, traditional remedies that meet the requirements are selectedand are approved as medicines to treat specific ailments.

In China The majority of Chinese don't view TCM as well as Western medicine as in conflict. In the event of emergency or extreme circumstances there is no doubt about making use of the standard Western medicine. However, the belief in Chinese medicine is still strong particularly in regards to maintaining the health of patients. For instance, when a person has been diagnosed as having acute appendicitis they consult a Western doctor, but they may also exercise or take Chinese herbs to ensure that the body is healthy enough to avoid appendicitis, or to speed up recovery after operation. A majority of Western medical practitioners in China don't reject the tradition of Chinese medicine, and utilize some elements of Chinese medicine in their own practices.

Certain hospitals use the combination with Chinese and Western treatments to treat diseases. For instance, medical professionals at Shanghai Cancer hospital evaluate patients in a collaborative manner and treat them with the traditional Chinese herbal formulas along with radiosurgery and Western medications. It is important to note that the application in Western medical treatment in China is quite unique with respect to the West. Contrary to the West There are only a few health professionals who practice routinely prescribed medical treatments or even to try methods like massage or physical therapy.

Additionally, Chinese specialists of Western medicine have not been influenced by the patterns of the West which promote empowerment of patients by recognizing the patient as a person as instead of an organ collection, and to ignore the patient when is appropriate. Chinese specialists of Western medicine have been examined for prescribing excessive amounts of medication, like corticosteroids and anti-infection drugs for typical viral diseases. It's likely that the prescriptions that are in the majority of cases known for their ineffectiveness against viral infections and illnesses will not provide much more help for patients than conventional Chinese herbs.

Modernization has also impacted the usage of TCM. There has been a social shift towards Western medical practices among young and educated people. They view TCM as a dated as well as a flimsy, non-scientific and superstiti practice. Students who attend TCM schools are often tempted to choose for non-TCM careers in Western medical services following their graduation. The shift to Western medical practices could be due to people's hectic lifestyles. There are those who believe that people do not have the time to make regular visits or to prepare herbal remedies at their own home. Despite the changes in society there are still a lot of people who look for TCM due to the fact that it's attractive and has a personal and comfortable patient-patient compliance.

Traditional medical practices are regarded as secondary in China. But, herbal medicine exercise like Qigong and other medicinal foods are still popular in China. Traditional medicine is generally less expensive than visiting hospitals for treatment. The government also encourages the practice of using traditional medicine. Acupuncture techniques or moxibustion as well as cupping are all practiced in certain regions of China. In general, a lot of individuals are now turning to the modern medical facilities to receive treatment.

Chapter 9: Chinese Religions and Culture

Since the beginning of time Chinese people China have always been a part of various faiths. In the present, there are five major religions followed in China which include Buddhism, Taoism, Confucianism, Islam, and Christianity. Apart from Islam and Christianity The "religions" that are practiced in China don't have faith in any one god (Taoists actually believe in, or at least adhere to hundreds of) Instead they have their own set of tenets they adhere to in order to ensure they live a moral life.

Buddhism

Introduced into China over 2 centuries ago, the majority all Chinese people have embraced Buddhism as a religion. Buddhism and divided it into three parts that are which are the Han, Tibetan, and Southern Buddhist religions. Buddhism is more than a religion, it's an entire cultural system. Buddhism has had a profound influence on Chinese literature, art and beliefs in at least one form or shape. In the present, there are around 13,000 Buddhist temples scattered across the Chinese landscape. Within the midst of them are over 180,000 monks and nuns that are determined to keep their tradition in a state of preservation.

Confucianism

Confucianism isn't a true religion, per se however it is more of an philosophical and moral system. The Confucian school of thought arose from the wisdom of the old Chinese philosophical Confucius (Kung Fu Tzu) which is why it's called. The belief of Confucius was that the only way to a peaceful and harmonious state was looking back in the past, to the lives of Sage Emperors. He believes that each person is a part of the world, and he should be a part of the society in a way.

One of the most fundamental principles of Confucianism refers to the relation between father as well as his son. Sons must always respect and respect their fathers. However fathers should try to be an honorable and exemplary man worthy of their sons to be respected. If everyone adheres to this one tenet, the society in general will function smoothly.

Taoism (Daoism)

The Taoist movement was founded with Lao Tzu, Taoism means "The Way," just like Confucianism is a philosophy which teaches people to lead their lives with integrity. The followers of Taoism adhere to the principles of Lao Tzu as outlined within the Tao Te Ching. Taoism believes that there exists an underpinning harmony throughout the world, and that one must do the best to avoid bringing imbalance. As per Taoist experts, there must always be an equilibrium between good and evil as well as between light and dark. There should be no need to be in a position to keep equilibrium within the world.

Islam as well as Christianity

Islam as well as Christianity are, without doubt, the two main religions in China. Even though Islam was present in China over 1,000 years ago, thanks to the interactions with Muslims on the Silk Road, it is still among the smallest religions in China with only 1.5-4 percent of China's total population.

Christianity On the contrary, is seeing an explosive growth in the number of Christians in the wake of the fall of Cultural Revolution and the opening China's borders to foreign influences. More over 26 million Chinese are Christians.

Each of these religions played a role in creating China the country it is today - an economic superpower that is rapidly growing yet it remains a clinging to their ancient beliefs and diverse cultural traditions.

The Chinese Culture

Due to its long tradition, China has a rich cultural heritage. Artists are a key factor in the transformation of any culture. Chinese cultural practices are no exception; China has produced many amazing artists over the period of its history. We'll take a look at several of the most famous artists in this chapter:

Ai Weiwei - Visual Artist

Ai Weiwei was born in 1957 in Beijing. He is a well-known Chinese contemporary visual artist as well as a political activist. He is a champion of the new generation of Chinese experimental artists.

Wang Guangyi - A renowned painter

Wang Guangyi is a renowned artist from Beijing. His work is complex and blends China's past heroics with the present materialistic style. An incredible twist of irony gives his paintings an unique flavour.

Xu Bing - Contemporary Artist

Xu Bing was born in 1955 in Beijing. He is a contemporary artist known for his dazzling large-scale installation pieces as well as his unique prints that explore the imaginative use of words and their powerful influence on understanding the world that we inhabit.

Zeng Fanzhi (1964) - One of the most financially rewarded artists

Zeng Fanzhi (1964) is an outstanding figure among the most popular Chinese contemporary artists. He is one of Asia's most profitable commercial artists, renowned for his stunning representations that are influenced with his physical as well as emotional physical and emotional conditions.

Zhao Bandi - The Panda Man

Zhao Bandi (1966), popularly referred to as the panda man is a highly regarded contemporaneous Chinese visual artist who is recognized for his well-known witty artworks, which include sketches, sculptures and clothes adorned with panda bears. The acclaimed collection of comic-like photographs, called Zhao Bandi and the Panda which features him in conversation with a stuffed panda bear via speech bubbles, humorously addresses serious issues in contemporary China including drug use, air pollution unemployment and even the ferocity.

Luo Zhongli - Capturing Rural China

Luo Zhongli (1948) is one of the most acclaimed contemporary Chinese artists, well-known for his vivid sketches of Chinese workers and paintings which vividly capture rural life of China.

Chen Yifei - An Oil Painter

Chen Yifei (1946-2005) was a well-known Chinese painter who was also one of the most important artists. He was a pioneer in Chinese oil paintings. Yifei is famous for his stunning realistic sketches of traditionally dressed melancholic Chinese women as well as captivating landscapes from his Chinese countryside. When he arrived in Shanghai at the end of the 20th century Chen Yifei crafted several of his greatest work, including a superb exquisitely painted collection that depicts impressionistic Chinese landscapes.

Ren Hang- A Bold Artist

Ren Hang is a bold visual artist hailing from Beijing. He is well-known for his explicit photos. His apparently explicit and sexually unambiguous works that are brimming with naked bodies and body parts that are private reveal the artist's extraordinary ability to manage nakedness that is desexualized and transforms human bodies into captivating artworks and sculptures that he captures by his camera.

Actors and composers

Music is a universal language that isn't bound by any borders. China provided many famous musicians to world. They did not just have significant influence on Chinese music, but also the entire world. Here are a few most famous composers from China (most are belong in the early twentieth century):

Benjamin Lees (1924-2010) was born in Harbin. He composed film scores and one of his most famous film score was Man Alive!

Chet Lam, a pianist, composer and conductor. His most famous works include: I'm Not What You Are Looking For, McDull^! Prince de la Bun

Danny Chan (1958-1993) was an artist, musician actor, composer, and singer who was who was born in Hong Kong. The credits include Gui ma fei ren, An Autumn's Tale.

Gillian Chung is a songwriter as well as model, actor, composer, and performer who hails from Hong Kong. She is most well-known for The Twins Effect, Love on the Rocks, Ip Man: The Final Fight, House of Fury, The Twins Effect II.

Joseph Koo was born in Guangzhou. He is among the most well-known composers of Hong Kong. His most well-known works include A Better Tomorrow, Fist of Fury, Fist of Legend, Return of the Dragon.

Kenny Bee was born in Hong Kong. Miracles, Initial D, The Chinese Feast, My Heart Is That Eternal Rose as well as Moon Warrior belong to his credits.

Mark Lui is a film score composer from Hong Kong. In addition to composing, he's additionally a designer and music producer and songwriter and musician. His most notable works include The Legend, Gorgeous, Last Hero in China, Crime Story, An Empress and the Warriors.

Melissa Hui is a Canadian composer who was born in Hong Kong. Her most well-known composition can be seen in Sunrise Over Tiananmen Square.

Nicholas Tse was born in Hong Kong. In addition to composing, he's an entrepreneur, record producer and musician as well as a singer-songwriter. Police Story, Shaolin

Soccer, New Police Story, Bodyguards and Assassins, Dragon Tiger Gate are among his most famous work.

He was born Qigang in Shanghai. His most famous work is The Flowers of War, Under the Hawthorn Tree.

Sam Hui is a widely known film score composer music producer and record maker musician, and singer-songwriter. His most famous work includes Swordsman, Winner Takes All, The Dragon from Russia, Games Gamblers Play, and Aces Go Places.

Teddy Robin Kwan was born in Guilin. He composes film scores and record producer, as well as a musician and singer-songwriter as well as film producer. Full Contact, Black Mask, Twin Dragons, City on Fire, Detective Dee: Mystery of the Phantom Flame are among his accomplishments.

The artist Xian Xinghai(1905-1945) was born in Macau. His most famous work was Song at Midnight.

Chapter 10: Famous tourist attractions

China is a country with a long history as well as a vast territory, which means there are many tourist spots. There are a lot of locations to explore, however taking in all of them in the course of a single trip is quite difficult. Let's take a look some of the spots that are considered must-see tourist destinations in China.

Great Wall of China in Beijing (Ten Thousand Li Long Wall)

Great Wall of China is not just the longest and largest wall on earth, also has a long and rich history and provides a breathtaking perspective. While the wall extends from the western part of China up to the eastern coastline (5000 kms) it is often referred to as the portion that is near Beijing when talking about China's Great Wall. It is the best-preserved portion of the wall that is characterized by mountain peaks that are steep, rugged landscape and breathtaking landscape. The wall has earned its place in "The seven wonders that are new to the Earth" as well as it is a UNESCO World Heritage site.

The Terracotta Army in Xi'an (Emperor Qin's Buried Battalions)

An amazing archaeological site that has been beneath the earth for over 2000 years. The Terracotta Army was discovered when farmers were drilling a well back in the year 1974. The site was included on the lists of World Cultural Heritage by 1987.

Underground army believed to have been crafted from Qin, the First Emperor Qin back during the Warring States Period (475 - 221 BC). The army has significant significance as it was able to triumph over other Chinese army. You may be wondering why they made an army similar to this one. According to legend, the Emperor Qin desired an army that would protect his body in the afterlife. He believed that these statues would be brought back to life after death and maintain the status of his emperor as they were during his life. The place is worth a visit and it is claimed that no trip to Xi'an or China is complete without a visit to the Terracotta Army.

The Forbidden City of Beijing (Imperial Palais for the 24 Emperors)

The name "Forbidden City" will surely be intriguing. It's called that because it was the 'Palace City' in which citizens were not permitted to be allowed to. It was as an Imperial palace nearly six centuries up to 1911. In 1911, the Ming as well as the Qing Dynasties (a total of 24 emperors) have made this palace their residence. The palace is now known as the Palace Museum', which is a treasure trove of Chinese cultural and historical relics. The palace is home to approximately 8000 rooms that are classically designed with golden roofs that are painted red and yellow. The palace was named as one of the top five palaces around the globe.

The Li River in Guilin (Watery Wonder)

The scenery around Li River is stunning. Li River is karst; it has attracted artists from all over the world. The beauty of the scenery makes the Li River a popular photographer's destination. While it is true that the Li River stretches over a vast expanse however, the 83-kilometer section of the river that runs that runs between Guilin to Yangshuo is one of the most beautiful. The body of water is surrounded by cliffs steep as well as stunning hills and rural villages that have bamboo grooves running all the way along the. According to National Geographic Magazine, Li River is listed among one of the "Top 10 Water Wonders" around the globe.

The Yellow Mountains in Huangshan (A Top National Park)

It is the Yellow Mountain Scenic Area in east China located near Shanghai and Hangzhou attracts tourists from all over the globe. The five unique views provide sunrises clouds, the sea of clouds deformed rocks, hot springs and twisted pine forests. National Park is one of the busiest in China and the Yellow Mountains are the most popular mountains in China.

The two other national parks in China are worth mentioning too. Jiuzhaigou National Park in the western part of Sichuan is known for its fall foliage and multi-colored lakes . Zhangjiajie National Forest Park is well-known for its beautiful rock pillars. The National

Parks are well worth a visit and offer unforgettable experiences.

Giant Pandas in Chengdu (National Treasure of China)

Giant Panda is one of the most beloved animals in the world. Zoos are everywhere throughout China as well as the rest of the world, where Giant Panda can be seen; Chengdu is the best location to view them since it is their home town.

In three different locations In three distinct locations, giant Pandas are visible in close proximity: Chengdu Panda Breeding and Research Center, Bifengxia Panda Base as well as Dujiangyan Panda Valley.

Chengdu Panda Center is in the northern part of the city and is a well-established center. Bifengxia Panda Base can be found two hours away from Chengdu and Pandas are seen in their natural surroundings in this area. Dujiangyan Panda Valley is an hour's drive from Chengdu. It is possible to get even nearer to Pandas by visiting this site.

The Potala Palace in Lhasa (Symbol of Tibet)

The palace contains an extensive quantity of books about Tibetan culture, history art, culture, and. The exquisite sculptures, sacred scriptures murals, Buddhist sculptures and antiques and the religious jewelry that are in the palace are inspiring for both travelers and pilgrims alike. The summer months are the best time to visit Tibet since Tibet is a plethora of festivals during this season. The site was made as a UNESCO World Cultural Heritage Site in 1994.

The Bund in Shanghai (International Architecture)

Bund is considered to be the most recognizable architectural icon of Shanghai. It features colonial European structures and towers. Huangpu District in Shanghai has been named one of the top business districts in the world.

The first British firm opened its doors in the Bund Shanghai, it was a renowned symbol of class. Shanghai was the most prosperous area throughout the late 18th and 19th centuries.

Victoria Harbor in Hong Kong (Best Bird's Eye View Place)

The view from the peak of Victoria Harbor to the people of Hong Kong is like the perspective Chinese tourists get after climbing to the Great Wall (not literally of course!). The top offers the best perspective of Hong Kong. The view is captivating at any time of the day, and at night. Buildings that rise high in the bustling Victoria Harbor stretching to mainland China can be observed in the expansive views during the day. The view from nighttime is breathtaking with the lights of different structures enticing the eye.

West Lake in Hangzhou (Paradise on Earth)

Chapter 11: Chinese Traditional Folktales

Like every other country, China has a vast collection of myths and folktales that they have collected over the years. They may appear to be fairy tales for children, but in reality is that they are books of literature that have been handed through generations.

Ho Kwan and the Ants

There was one man known as Ho Kwan from a village known as Kuang Nan. Ho Kwan was a kind and compassionate individual and so kind that he didn't harm any living thing. Ho Kwan was not a rich person however, he was wealthy. He was known for placing his money in a jar before putting it inside a casket to keep it safe. However, white ants, among them plenty of them in his village got into the casket and devoured an enormous amount of silver.

Ho Kwan's family discovered that they had been there, they followed the insects back to their nest that was a huge cavern. They believed that if they could collect all the ants, and then place them all in a crucible they might be able get back some of the silver they consumed. If Ho Kwan heard about their idea, he advised the group not to go the idea as it was too much for him to imagine killing the ants because they ate a portion of his wealth.

The next at night Ho Kwan dreamt about an enormous army of soldiers in white, requesting Ho Kwan to board an automobile so that he could meet their King. Ho Kwan was taken into an upscale city. When his carriage departed and court officials greeted the man and took him to the palace of the royal family at the heart of town.

The king walked out of the doorway to greet Ho Kwan, and the King told Ho Kwan that his kindness has saved thousands of his subjects from the dreadful fate of death. At that point, Ho Kwan knew that he was talking to the king white ants, those whom he had saved previously. The king was very happy with Ho Kwan's actions that Ho Kwan instructed Ho Kwan to dig at the root on one of his trees that were on his yard; think of it as an ant's present to him.

When he woke up the following day, Ho Kwan headed to the tree the ants warned him about and began digging. After digging for about two minutes, he discovered an enormous jar filled with silver, gold and other precious metals. Because of his generosity and the kindness of white ants, Ho Kwan and his family could live rich lives.

The Goddess of Silkworms

the Emperor of China was married to a gorgeous woman named Si-ling who was a love of his heart. Because he was a generous ruler, people adored the Emperor as well as his compassionate wife.

In the past, people wore clothing made from the furs of creatures they hunted. But, the animals that roam the forest have become scarce, and have deprived the people of the raw materials they needed to create their clothing. In the court of Emperor Si-ling and other members, racked their heads to come up with how to assist the people. Si-ling was disappointed that she was unable to help her husband in his troubles.

The emperor along with his spouse were strolling around the Imperial garden. As they were walking , they discussed the problems facing the people. The Emperor was struck by some worms within the Mulberry tree. He observed that they seemed to be spinning some sort of thread. Si-ling sat and looked around, and she was also fascinated of the fact that they were able to contain enough thread to form their own cocoons.

One day later, Si-ling visited the emperor, and she said she was likely to make use of the threads from Mulberry worms to create clothes for the masses. The emperor asked how she would unwind the thread from cocoons. He's attempted to do it previously but the thread would break. Si-ling assured him that she'd find an avenue to gather enough string in order to create cloth.

Si-ling tried unwinding the string with her hands, but as she anticipated it, the threads were too fragile. Then she realized that it would be much easier to soften the cocoons slightly before the thread could be unraveled. After several trials Si-ling discovered that she was able to unravel the threads , it was much more easy. Then she thought about who could create their own cloth and threads by using cocoons from the silkworm. This resulted in her being referred to as"the "Goddess of the Silkworm."

From that point on there was no need to think about where to find the materials they needed for their clothes and now had an almost endless amount of materials thanks to tiny silkworms and their tiny homes.

These are only a few of the many interesting and fascinating tales that came from the culture of ancient China. Similar to the folktales that originated from the West The majority of older Chinese stories also contained life lessons. This is most likely the way kids were taught morality and proper conduct.

Chapter 12: Story of China as well as United Kingdom Relationship

China has a long background in its place in the British Isles that stretch back to the period during the Ming Dynasty during the early 17th century. Actually, China was once a part of the British Empire. This is why there was a lot of interaction between the two nations that have both developed into world power during the 20th century. To fully comprehend the deepness of the connection between the two countries, it's crucial to look back to the 17th century.

17th Century: In the Ming Dynasty

Though interactions between English and Chinese occurred prior to during the Ming Dynasty, they were very few and far between. Actually, the recorded historical records only record a handful of meetings between the inhabitants of both countries. It was only in the 17th century that it could be stated that the seeds of the friendship were planted. Of course, in this time there was no United Kingdom did not exist in fact, it was a time when the British Empire had just begun. So, in all of the British Isles, it was the English who are believed to have met the Chinese first.

In the 1620s ships from England were sailing to Macau. At the time, Macau was leased to Portugal by China. The English merchant ship, The Unicorn, sank close to the island. The cannon of the ship was dumped to be used by Portuguese and then sold to China. It was then that the Chinese began to replicate the weapons under the name Hongqiao.

On the 27th June 1637 the first contact between Chinese as well as the British could be believed to have happened. The captain John Wendell led 4 heavily equipped vessels to Macao to attempt to make trade more open in China as well as England. They were not component that of the East India Company. They were, instead, an individual group, whose leader was named Sir William Courteen and had been granted PS10,000 for the personal interests of the King Charles I.

The Portuguese reached an arrangement with Chinese to safeguard Macao and were able to do so. However, they were able to create a stir among those who were the Ming authorities. The following summer year The English captured some of Bogue forts. For some weeks, they were engaged in smuggling and lower-level fights. The English were forced to seek assistance from the Portuguese after three of their members were held hostage. Following this incident, they departed their home on the Pearl River on the 27th of December. However, the story isn't certain if they were able to return to home.

1644-1991: Qing Dynasty

At the time at this point, it was clear that the British Empire was already on the verge of being one of the strongest empires that the world has ever witnessed. Naturally it did not take too long for China to be influenced by the Empire.

When he arrived in 1685, Shen Fung-Tsung became the first Chinese from China to travel to Britain. He was changed into Catholicism within China and was brought to Europe. He also was able to get an appointment in Paris with

Louis XIV of France. He was later taken for a meeting with the King James II.

In 1793 in 1793, the Mccartney Embassy was inaugurated in 1793. It was headed by George Macartney, this was the first diplomatic mission of Britain that went to China. The mission had many objectives. the mission, the most significant ones were opening ports in China for trade with the British and the establishment of an permanent British Embassy in Beijing as well as the lifting on trade barriers in Guangzhou. The delegation was able to have a meeting to meet with Qianlong Emperor, however all requests made by the British were turned down. Even with the loss however, the trip was extremely beneficial. The records of the geographic, political as well as cultural takeaways made by members of China were large.

1839-1842 the First Opium War

In the early 1820s, Lintin Island located in the Pearl River estuary was transformed by British merchants into a hub of the trade in opium. This was crucial because it was later utilized by drug smugglers who brought enough opium from China to be arouse the authorities. It was among the main reasons for an outbreak of the First Opium War.

The conflict was waged between the Qing Dynasty of China and the British Empire. The primary cause of the war could be attributed to the differing views regarding the trade and diplomatic relationship and the system of justice that was in place in China for foreigners.

There was a huge demand Chinese items like silk, tea and porcelain was incredibly large on the European market between the 17th and 18th century. But, it led to unbalanced trade since in China there was no market available for European products was largely not even existent. China was self-sufficient and didn't have a need for imports from other countries. Additionally the Qing dynasty did not allow the Europeans to enter the inside of China. In the mid-point to the end of 18th century the Canton system was established. This system ensured that the entire sea trade that involved foreigners was restricted within in the Canton region.

These circumstances made it extremely difficult for European merchants to recover the gold they had used on Chinese products. In the end, however, it was clear that the British East India Company was able to hold an exclusive right to British trade. It was in a position take action to stop it. It began auctioning of the opium was grown in its plantations across India. Foreign traders who were independent bought the opium for silver, which merchants needed. The opium was then transported on the Chinese coast to be sold to local middlemen in charge of the sale within China.

Silver started flowing back into the bank accounts from the East India Company while the number of addicts to opium in China began to increase. This certainly frightened authorities in China. Chinese authorities. Daoguang Emperor refused to accept plans for legalization and taxation of opium in 1839. However, Lin Zexu was appointed viceroy to end the trade. About 20,000 opium sacks were taken by Lin. It was that there was a loss of about 1210 tons, as there was no compensation. The trade was slowed down by the merchants from abroad who were confined to their homes.

The British government did not explicitly claim the right of China to regulate the importation of this drug. However they did protest the sudden confiscation of drug. They took action that were a form of war, which was referred to in the First Opium War. Through its gunnery and naval power they British could cause havoc with the Chinese and secured the war with a decisive victory.

The British victory resulted in the Treaty of Nanking in 1842. It was one of the first unequal treaties, as the Chinese would later refer to them. In accordance with the conditions of the treaty Britain was given indemnity. 5 ports under the treaty were opened, and Hong Kong Island was ceded to the British. In 1843, the Treaty of Bogue in 1843 added to this treaty in that it provided extraterritoriality for British subjects living in China in China. Britain was awarded the highest priority status for a nation.

The Treaty of Nanking was most certainly generous to the British but it was not capable to meet the imperial goals of strengthening trade and diplomatic relations. In the end, it was an element in an event known as the

Second Opium War. In addition this war is thought to be the beginning of the modern Chinese history in China.

1856-1860 Second Opium War

As we mentioned previously as well, as mentioned earlier, the Treaty of Nanking was not suitable with the British. In addition, acts of agression continued to be committed in the face of the British. In 1847 an Expedition to Canton took place in the wake of one of these acts. The 1850s were a time when Western imperialism increased quickly. The powers of the west shared the desire to expand their market in the overseas world and to create new ports of entry.

At this time the treaties would usually contain a clause that allowed the treaty to be renegotiated within 12 years. This is why the British called for a renegotiation the Treaty of Nanking with the Qing authorities. They also cited the most popular nation status to negotiate. For the demands made by British were huge. They wanted all of China to be opened to merchant companies from Britain and also legalization of the trade in opium. They also wanted the trade in coolies to be controlled too. The British also demanded permission to have an official from the British ambassador to live in Beijing. They also demanded that they should have the English translation of treaties should prevail over treaties that are which were written in Chinese language.

The war's beginning can be traced back to a cargo vessel named Arrow. The ship was seized by Chinese marines, who believed it was a piracy vessel. Because the vessel had been registered with the British The marines wanted the crew to be released as well as an apology. Three crew members were let go. The Chinese decision to not release them was a source of anger for the British. They took on Canton in 1856. fights being conducted in sporadic intervals until 1857 when British returned in Hong Kong.

Following a delay caused by the parliamentary vote as well as an election general, British began to look for alliances in their war against China. The empire couldn't afford to spend all its resources because of the Indian Mutiny in 1857. The Americans as well as the Russians did not agree, however the French took it upon being informed of complaints by their ambassador in China.

The first phase of the war ended in 1858 when the signature of the Treaty of Tientsin by Lord Elgin. There were four sections of the treaty that were signed by each of the participants. Other than Britain other participants included France and the US and Russia. The primary consequence of the treaty resulted in more ports became open to European powers as well as the US to trade.

Although the treaty brought the peace of China, it proved also short and insecure. The Court's ministers convinced the Xianfeng Emperor to resist the growing power of the Western power in the month of June. The result was being the Second Battle of Taku Forts. After the Indian revolt was quelled, Britain was free to increase its troops in China. In the year 1859, The Third Battle of Taku Forts took place resulting in an British victory. In the month of October, 1860, Anglo-French army occupied Beijing. After taking over the Summer Palaces, they destroyed them on the direction by Lord Elgin.

The Second Opium War soon came to an end when the Convention of Beijing on 18th October, 1960. Britain gained Kowloon and the trade in opium was made legal.

1912-1949: War Years

In this time the rise of communism took hold in China which led to the downfall of the last imperial monarchy the Qing dynasty in 1912. In 1912, the Republic of China was formed from the result.

As of 1916, Chinese workers were lent to British as a means of aid to help them during the First World War. In 1917, China became a member of with the United Kingdom and the Allies to fight in the war. Then, China enters into a war with Japan between 1937 and 1941. Although the British public backed China however, China decided to concentrate in the protection of Singapore and the British Empire. This meant that China was unable to provide any assistance other than providing training facilities and Air bases throughout India. In the Second World

War, China and Britain team up in the fight against Japan.

From 1949 until Present People's Republic of China

In the First World War, the Nationalist Chinese government was strongly anti-communist, and was allying itself with Britain. Following the conflict, Britain tried to take steps to stabilize China to protect its interests. Although it was not able to interfere with Chinese issues because of the accord of 1945 in Moscow agreement however, it did support the nationalists.

It was discovered in the month of august 1948 when the communist organization gained popularity throughout the country and was winning more battles. This led to British officials British began to plan for a takeover by the communists. As of January, 1950 Britain became one of the nations to officially recognize China as the People's Republic of China, however, it retained a monopoly on Hong Kong. It wasn't until 1997 when Britain finally handed over Hong Kong's sovereignty to China. Hong Kong to China.

Tensions among the two countries were a constant for a lengthy period of time. In the last century, it was the only time when the two countries formed an enmity. Trade agreements that amount to millions of pounds have been reviewed and concluded. They also pledged greater military collaboration. Xi Jinping, the current Chinese President, has had a meeting with the Queen Elizabeth II.

Quiz

You think you're now an expert on Sino-English relations? So why not give this test a shot and see if you can pass?

1. What year was it when The First Opium War take place?

2. What year was it when it happen that the Second Opium War take place?

3. What happened to what happened to the Second Opium War end?

4. What were the relationships among China as well as Britain in the World Wars?

Chapter 13: Story of Chinese Relationship with the Soviet and Russia

The relations with China and Russia go back many years. Actually the relationship been a key factor in shaping the country to the nation it is today. In this regard, the relationship of these two nations is one worth knowing.

The Early History

Although China as well as Russia are separated only via land truth lies in the fact that their very first official gathering took place in 1640. Both regions were continuously attacked by steppe nomads. It was a time when both were subjugated to the rule by the Mongols. Therefore it was assumed that there would not be any contact between them.

In 1640 Cossacks in 1640 from Siberia ended within The Amur Basin. At the time, Amur Basin was under the rule under the Manchus who were set to begin their assault on China. In 1689, the Russians were defeated in 1689 and a Russo-Chinese border was drawn up through the Treaty of Nerschinsk. Relations between the two nations were difficult due to the lack of mutual understanding. There no common language that could help facilitate discussions. In addition was that the Chinese were keen to treat Russians as barbarians who were their tributary.

Relations Until 1917

In the 1750s In the 1750s, it was the time that the Chinese Empire gained the control of Xinjiang. For the Russian Empire however, it was able to extend into Kazakhstan in the middle into the nineteenth century. In this way both countries shared their borders crossing in the present Western Xinjiang and eastern Kazakhstan. Through the Treaty of Kuja in 1851 it was authorized trade between the two nations.

In the Second Opium War, saw China becoming weaker. However, Russia kept increasing its power. Russia was able to take over the north bank of Amur River and expanded their control over the coastline up to the Korean border with the help of several agreements. By 1870, Russia had control over Ili. The

Qing dynasty was determined to retake the region, however there were a number of other factors that led to Russia abandoning its claims on the area. In 1881, the Treaty of St Petersburg saw the Qing dynasty reclaiming the region that was disputed.

From the time of this treaty until 1917, there were various relations between these two nations. However, they were less importance when both countries were undergoing an era of unrest in the civil sphere. There was a civil war in both countries. Qing Dynasty of China was dismantled by nationalists in 1912, and this led to the establishment of the Republic of China. In Russia the Tsarist Dynasty was ended by the February Revolution in 1917.

The Modern Age

The relations that existed between Russia and China following 1917 was characterized by the rising of communism in both countries. There were some significant incidents that affected both countries prior to communism coming into the spotlight.

In the Russian Civil War, the government of China joined in the Allied intervention by deploying troops. This was on the basis of the Chinese community throughout North Russia and Siberia. Regions in Tuva and Mongolia were declared to be contested territories. In 1924 Mongolia was declared the Mongolian People's Republic became created by Mongolian rebels, who were under the leadership of Damdin Sukhbaatar. He was backed by Soviet troops and his government was strongly pro-Soviet.

Prior to it, the Chinese Civil War

In 1921 in 1921, The Kuomintang (also known as known as the Nationalist Party of China started receiving support from the Soviet Union. In 1923 it was reported that the Communist Party of China was given instructions by the Comintern to sign a formal military agreement in conjunction with that of the Nationalist Party. But, Chiang Kai-shek, the leader of the Kuomintang was able to remove all of his Soviet advisors. He also put limitations on the participation of members of the Communist Party in the government. In 1927 it was reported that the

Communist Party was purged by Chiang out of the alliance. The result was being the Chinese Civil War.

The Chinese Civil War would continue until 1950, just a few months after the founding of the People's Republic of China by Mao Zedong. In the time of the civil war the Soviet did provide some help towards China's Communist Party of China. However, they suffered with a devastating loss in 1934 when the Kuomintang took over China's Chinese Soviet Republic. It was also the beginning of the Long March of the Communist Party of China to Shaanxi.

In the Second Sino-Japanese War

The Empire of Japan conducted a successful invasion of Manchuria in 1931. They established a puppet state called Manchukuo by 1932. This marked the beginning of the Second Sino-Japanese War. One month after the incident in the Marco Polo Bridge Incident in 1937, a non-aggression treaty was signed through both the Soviet Union with the Republic of China.

In during the Second World War, both China as well as China and the Soviet

Union end up taking huge losses. Actually, they both suffered the most losses compared to other nations during the war. China suffered over 15 million of its citizens during the Second Sino-Japanese War. It was estimated that the Soviet Union lost 27 million people during the war.

On August 8th 1945 on the 8th of August 1945, the Soviet attack on Manchuria was officially launched. It was only three months later than the fall to Nazi Germany. It was also the time in which the bombings at Hiroshima and Nagasaki occurred. The military operations in Manchuria was an enormous one which resulted in that the Soviet Union sending in 1.5 million soldiers. They fought 1 million soldiers of the Kwantung Army, the last Japanese presence of the military in Manchuria.

It is believed that the Kwantung Army took significant causalities while the Soviet forces continued to win an overwhelming victory. 700,000 Japanese soldiers surrendered. The weapons was the Soviet Union captured from the Kwantung Army were distributed to the Communist Party of

China. They would later use them by the Communist Party would later use these weapons during the Chinese Civil War.

In the War of Liberation

The Communist Party of China began to gain popularity with the Chinese people in 1946. Between 1946 and 1950, there was a War of Liberation can say to have occurred. It was mostly an People's war. In the course of this time, the Kuomintang was becoming increasingly isolated. They made an unintentional attempt to stop corruption and implement popular reforms.

Mao Zedong proclaimed the People's Republic of China on the 1st October 1949. In 1949, the Civil War came to an conclusion in May 1950 during Kuningtou. Battle of Kuningtou. In the aftermath of the fight that ended in the Kuomintang was forced to leave Mainland China. However, they maintained the control of Taiwan.

When China was established as China, also known as the People's Republic of China, the supreme authority in politics of China as well as that of the Soviet Union came under the rule of communism. Both of the ruling parties adhered to the Marxist-Leninist doctrine.

The Sino-Soviet Split

Since both countries adhered to the same ideology following the declaration of the PRC The Soviet Union and China became the most close of allies. They began to cooperate. Soviets began to offer designs, equipment and skilled workers to assist in the modernization and industrialization in the People's Republic of China. The level of support was certainly not minimal. However, it was lower than the expectations of Chinese. In the 1960s, relationship between the two countries were strained after the Sino-Soviet split. The result was the Sino-Soviet border war.

The Sino-Soviet Split arose mainly out of the differing ideologies between both communist groups. When China was considering a peaceful coexistence with the Soviet Union, Soviet Union was considering the possibility of peaceful coexistence with the West, China, under Mao Zedong, was considering the possibility of a hostile approach. That is to say the two countries were trying gain control of the direction the worldwide communist movement was likely to follow. The breakup in both the USSR as well as China was among the most significant events to happen in the Cold War. There was a possibility of war between these two countries at some moment in the time.

In the midst of the conflict there was a border war that had not been declared. occurred within the borders of the two nations in the year 1969. Border crossings were closed or subjected to severe restrictions. The same as both countries strengthened their security at their borders. The border between them became an extremely militarized and fortified zone. There were nuclear missile sites constructed on both sides of the border.

Relations with China ended after the passing of Mao Zedong. After Mao Zedong's Gang of Four was overthrown by the PRC's successive leaders, the PRC were able to soften their attitudes towards China and Soviet Union. The relationship was improved after the visit of Mikhail Gorbachev in 1989 to Beijing.

Post-Soviet relations with China and Russia

The Soviet Union was formally dissolved in 1991 by Mikhail Gorbachev, the last Soviet President. It certain to have had an enormous impact across the globe. It also proved beneficial to the relationship with China and the newly-formed country, Russia. Actually, the relations between the two countries was significantly improved following the year 1991.

Through the years the two countries have upgraded their relations at least three times. The most recent one came in 2001, when Russia together with China signed the Treaty of Good-Neighborliness and Friendly Cooperation.

Relations in Energy: Since its dissolution, the Soviet Union, the relations between China and Russia regarding energy issues have generally been cooperative. There is a shared respect for their mutual geopolitical and strategic interests. China's economy China is expanding rapidly which puts an increasing demand on China to secure energy imports. However the economics of Russia is mostly driven by the necessity to sell its own natural resources.

Although the energy relationships among the countries been generally positive over time however, they haven't been free of their fair share of problems. Both countries have made numerous announcements of their bilateral cooperation in energy. However the energy relationships between them are limited because of factors like price concerns and mutual suspicion. The infrastructure for transportation has been inadequate and both nations are trying to fight for influence within Eurasia.

Military Relations 1989: Tiananmen Square protests led to the enactment the arms embargo imposed by the EU over China. This led China to emerge as a trusted customer for exports of military equipment from Russia. In reality, exports to China was close to 50% of military exports to foreign markets of Russia. A five-year agreement on defense cooperation is signed in the year 1993 by the defense ministers from both countries. This enabled the number of military attaches based in both capitals to grow.

As it happens the relations among China and Russia could soon be changing. The rapid advancements in technology in China have led the country to develop the capability of manufacturing sophisticated military equipment and weapons. In reality, China can now produce warships and submarines. At present, China imports the equipment and machinery that it cannot manufacture by itself. In time it is anticipated that the capabilities of China will increase to the point where China no longer needs to depend on Russia.

Mutual Trade The most fascinating aspects of the Sino-Russian relationship is the fact that they trade in their respective national currencies. In the case of commercial transactions, currencies of both countries are utilized instead that of US Dollar. This was not just to strengthen the relationships among China as well as Russia however, but to offer security to their national economies in case a global financial crisis occurred.

As you can see, relationships with China with Russia are quite great and have come quite far from the tense Sino-Soviet divide. Of course it is still to be seen what the outcome will be of the relationship in the near future.

Chapter 14: On the relationship Between China as well as the United States

The relationship between the United States and China is one that everyone observes. In this type of relationship, each country tends to view each other as an potential adversary. Yet they view each other as an important strategic partner. It is generally believed that the Sino-American relationship is the most crucial bilateral relationship that exists today in this 21st century. It could be the one to shape the future of the entire world.

The relations between these two countries has generally been stable, however there were times when they were involved engaged in open war. A few notable instances include the Vietnam War and the Korean War. In the present there is a sense that China and the United States and China do have common interests in the security, economic and political areas. For instance there are shared concerns between the two countries in the area of expansion of nuclear weapons and the combating of terrorist acts.

It's fascinating to observe the way in which the relationship between two of the world's top powers has changed over time.

In the Qing Dynasty

The diplomatic formal relations among China with America United States can be traced back to 1844 when Qing Dynasty was in power. They began talks that culminated in the signing of Treaty of Wangxia.

Prior to this treaty, it was known that the United States was already engaged in commerce with Chinese. In 1842 there was the First Opium War took place which led to the Treaty of Nanking. As a result of the treaty various Chinese ports were forced available to trade with foreign European countries, particularly Britain. This was a risk to American interest within Chinese trade. In the end, the Treaty of Wangxia was a move to stop that from happening by providing American trading the same significance that it had British trade. At the time of the Second Opium War, there was a brief confrontation between Qing forces and American armies during the Battle of the

Barrier Forts. It was the first time in history that both countries had fought one another.

The 1800s The 1800s: The Chinese Exclusion Act

A number of events occurred in the 1800s that impacted the relations with China with China and the United States. in 1868 Anson Burlingame was provided by the administration of the Qing dynasty to be their ambassador for the US. This meant that Burlingame was able to travel around the USA to help build an alliance for the fair treatment of Chinese immigrants as well as China. His efforts led to the Burlingame Treaty of 1868.

However the most significant factor that affected Sino-American relations at this time is in the California Gold Rush. In this time an intercontinental railway was being constructed and also. There was a huge emigration of Chinese at this time also. They were employed on the railroad , and actually, they became the main workforce for the construction. However, the huge influx was a source of resentment for the majority of American citizens. The

Chinese were ostracized from mining. In the aftermath, many of them ended up living in Chinatowns situated in different cities, including San Francisco. They were forced to do jobs that paid low wages for cleaning, as well as managing restaurants.

In the late 1870s, the economy following the Civil War was in decline. In the same period anger toward Chinese was growing. Chinese began to take political significance through Denis Kearney, the leader of the Labor party. In addition to Kearney and the Labor group, John Bigler, the governor of California and the governor of California, also expressed anti-Chinese views. Both politicians put on the responsibility for slump in wage rates upon Chinese coolies. Chinese coolies.

China-haters reached their apex through the Chinese Exclusion Act which was adopted by Congress on 1882. This was the first major restriction on freedom of immigration throughout America's history. United States of America. It was passed in the wake of revisions of the Burlingame Treaty in 1880. In the wake of those changes, the United States became capable of temporarily suspending immigration. The Congress took action quickly to bring an end to the law, which allows Chinese migration to be temporarily suspended. Workers who are skilled and untrained from China are now barred from the US for up to 10 years. The punishment was jail time and deportation. The ban was extended many times and was eventually in effect for over 60 years.

The Boxer Rebellion

An uprising was sparked in the year 1899 by Chinese nationalists. They adopted the title from"the" Society of Right and Harmonious Fists. The society was the cause of the violent uprising in China that was later known as"the Boxer Rebellion by the Western nations. The rebellion was a protest against influence of foreigners in trade, politics and technology as well as religions. The campaigns were conducted between November 1899 to September 1901. This was in the final year of Manchu ruling in China during the Qing Dynasty.

The uprising began as an anti-imperialist, anti foreign movement that was a part of the peasants of northern

China. The revolt was a reaction to westerners taking over the land of indigenous Chinese. Westerners also made concessions to taking, as well as giving immunity to criminals for as long as he/ changed to
Catholicism. Revolutionaries targeted foreigners who were building railroads and who were not adhering to the rules in Feng Shui. They also slammed Christians since they believed they were accountable for the Western dominance over China.

On June 1, 1900 rebels invaded Peking. They destroyed the area in the vicinity of that of the foreign
Legations. On the 21st day of June The Empress Dowager declared war to all Western powers of China in reaction to the attack of foreign countries over the Chinese Dagu Forts. In the aftermath, the Siege of the International Legations was held during which all foreigners, diplomats as well as civilians and soldiers were surrounded. In fact, Chinese Christians were not spared.

The Western powers joined to create The Eight-Nation Alliance. The alliance was formed by France and Austria-Hungary Italy, Germany, Russia, Japan, the United States and Britain. They sent 20,000 soldiers to liberate their citizens. In the beginning the international forces fell during the battle of Langfang by an Chinese Muslim army. The second battle took place under the name of the Gaselee Expedition, and it proved to be a great success. But, this was mostly because of the internal conflicts present in China. Chinese forces.

In the wake of the defeat, in the aftermath of the war, the Chinese government was forced to compensate the victims. They were also required to make a variety of concessions. The reforms adopted following the Boxer rebellion played a key part in the end of the Qing Dynasty and the foundation of the Chinese Republic.

It is true that the United States was relegated to an insignificant role in the defeat of the Boxer Rebellion, but its contribution was important. This was due to its presence US vessels and troops which were stationed in the Philippines

The Chinese had to also pay the indemnities to each member of the alliance on their own. For instance, the United States received $11 million that it used to fund the promotion of cultural and academic trade with China. It also utilized the funds to assist in the modernization process of China. It also helped with the creation of numerous colleges across China such as those at the Tsinghua College in Peking.

It is the Open Door Policy

In the early 1890s, the world's major powers of the time began in the 1890s by creating spheres of influence that they could use for their own purposes in China. These comprised Britain, France, Japan, Germany, and Russia. At the time when China's Qing Dynasty was still in control. This arrangement was unsuitable for people in United States who demanded that this practice was halted so that all nations could be able to conduct business in China with equal rights.

John Hay, the US Secretary of State in 1899, wrote diplomatic letters to the countries. He asked them to ensure that the territorial and administrative sovereignty of China was protected. He also asked them to not hinder the use of the ports under treaty within their respective areas of influence. However, the states eluded their obligation. They claimed that it was impossible for them to accept any thing until they had given their approval. John Hay took this response as an acknowledgment of the idea. The plan has been referred to by the name of the Open Door Policy.

The Open Door Policy was respected worldwide, without doubt. However, it was not heeded in the case of Japan and Russia in their attempts to expand into the area of Manchuria. It was the United States did protest the actions of Russia but without success. Russia as well as Japan were eventually fighting in their way through the Russo-Japanese War of 1904. In 1904, the United States had to mediate peace between them.

Japan proved to be a second obstacle to the policy due to the Twenty-One Demands. This idea was first proposed in the then Republic of China in 1915. Secret agreements were also signed to the Allies in the name of Japan. Japan was promised territories that were owned by Germany in China. Japan attacked Manchuria in

1931, and then occupied Manchuria. The invasion is criticized by United States and other countries. It led to backing of the US for China after China went to war with Japan following the year 1937.

The relationship Between both the United States and the Republic of China

Governments of the United States recognized that the Republic of China government was the sole legitimate government for China following the Xinhai Revolution of 1911. This was in spite of having several governments that ruled over different regions of China. It was not until 1928, that China was united under a single , unifying government led by Kuomintang.

In during the Second World War

The Second Sino-Japanese War started in 1937. It was the year that United States began to provide assistance in China. Republic of China thanks to the US President, Franklin D. Roosevelt. In the past, in the US there were a number of Neutrality Acts were adopted and passed with the backing of isolationists. According to the Acts,

American aid could not be given to nations in war. However it was the Second Sino-Japanese War was undeclared. So, Roosevelt denied that China was at war and permitted the sending of aid to China.

In America the United States, the public was generated for the Chinese through reports from missionaries and other sources. There were also accounts of the brutality that occurred in China in the hands of the Japanese as well as those concerning Nanking Massacre. Nanking Massacre, which came to be referred to by the name of Rape of Nanking. Relations with America and Japan were further strained following the USS Panay incident. The incident involved an U.S. Navy gunboat which was accidentally sunk through Japanese aircraft. Roosevelt requested Japan to pay compensation as well as an apology. Even after they were granted but the relationship between the two countries continued to decline.

The relationship was ultimately destroyed in the month of December 1941 following the surprise attack carried out by Japanese Japanese in Pearl Harbor. Following the incident, massive amounts of aid were given to China through Roosevelt. Roosevelt administration. People were completely opposed to Japan following Pearl Harbor. In the aftermath of Pearl Harbor, US Congress also adopted amendments in the Chinese Exclusion Act. Roosevelt also made steps to ending the unjust treaties. Roosevelt also drafted his Treaty for Relinquishment of Extraterritorial Rights in China.

In all likelihood there was a perception that Chiang's Chinese government led by Chiang could not be capable of putting up an effective resistance against the Japanese. There was also the perception of Chiang was more concerned with fighting the communists than the Japanese. These views started to grow in importance. In America there was a smattering of oppositional views in relation to China. One group was looking to join with communists to prepare for a counter-offensive assault on China's Japanese mainland. Others sought air power and backed the position taken by Chiang.

In the Chinese Civil War

The conflict among China's Communist Party of China and the Republic of China kept increasing throughout the Second World War. Following the war's end these wars exploded into civil conflict. It was the time when Kuomintang lost control over mainland China following that Chinese Civil War which took place in 1949. In August of the same year it was the time that US State Department drafted the China White Paper.

In the white paper, in this white paper, the United States announced that it will be following a non-intervention policy towards Taiwan and the Republic of China based in Taiwan as well as to upcoming attack of the People's Liberation Army. Chiang Kai-shek and the Chinese military under his leadership must travel to Taiwan in order to accept an agreement to surrender Japan. This marked the beginning of the occupation by military of Taiwan.

The Relationship between the two during the Cold War

Following the outbreak of Korean War, the US government of President Truman continued to send economic and military assistance towards China. Republic of China. It was during this time that the Taiwan Strait was neutralized by the US along with its United States Seventh Fleet. This was done in order to stop the incursion into Formosa By Communist forces. In the meantime, United States kept providing the Republic of China with financial grants in accordance with the Foreign Assistance Act and other related Acts. Also, there was an Sino-American Mutual Defense Treaty between the two countries. The situation would persist until the day that the US officially acknowledged China as the People's Republic of China in 1979.

The end of diplomatic Relations

The 1st day of January 1979 The United States finally changed the diplomatic recognition of the Chinese nation to Beijing from Taipei by means of the U.S.-PRC Joint Communique. In the Joint Communique, the United States also recognized that the People's Republic of China is the country's government. China. In the Joint Communique that the people from America will ensure that the people of

United States will keep maintaining the cultural, commercial and other informal relations between Taiwan. Taiwanese people. Since the time it has been it has become the Republic of China is typically known as Taiwan to avoid confusion, even though Taiwan being the People's Republic of China claiming Taiwan as an independent province of China.

The relationship Between the US and China People's Republic of China

It is a fact that United States did not officially recognize the PRC for 30 years following the time it was founded. Instead the US continued to maintain diplomatic relations with the government it believed to be China's legitimate state. China that is, the Republic of China, based in Taiwan.

In the Korean War

The Korean started when the military that comprised China as well as China and the United States engaged in conflict out in the year 1950. North Korea also invaded South Korea with the assistance from the Soviets. In response to the invasion, it was decided that the United Nations Security Council was called to meet, and it approved UNSC Resolution 82. In it, war was declared against North Korea unanimously. The resolution was largely because of the Soviet Union which had boycotted all UN events since the beginning of this year.

The forces of the allied, led by America and America, were able to push against North Korea's army. North Korean army past the border. They began to move closer to the frontier that separated China as well as North Korea. This led China to make a huge intervention in the conflict by aiding North Korea.

The Korean War continued for two years, and finally came to an impasse. In 1953 The Korean Armistice Agreement was signed. Since since then, one of the most important aspects of relationship between the US and China has been the conflict over the Korea issue. The Chinese intervention during the Korean War also brought about significant changes in US policy regarding Taiwan. Instead of being given only a minimal amount of assistance, Taiwan was now being granted the status of having protection by Taiwan by the United States.

In the Vietnam War

China was involved with the Vietnam War in 1949 after it was reunited under regime of the communists. China was a part of the communist regime. People's Republic of China started providing training and support for communists who were operating in Vietnam. In 1962 the chairman Mao Zedong agreed that Hanoi would receive 90,000 rifles and guns by China at no cost whatsoever. China also began to supply anti-aircraft and engineering battalions. The engineering battalions assumed the responsibility of repairing the damages caused by America and also perform other important engineering works. This meant that the Vietnamese divisions were freed to continue fighting American troops. United States.

It's the Impasse in Relations

The United States kept working tirelessly to ensure that the People's Republic of China could not be able to take over the place that was originally reserved for China within the United Nations. It even urged its allies not to engage in any relations with China. People's Republic of China. In actual fact the PRC was subject to a trade embargo put in place for the PRC along with its surrounding countries, and urged to adhere to it.

The Thinning Of the Relations

The shift took place in the Sino-American relationship at the middle of the 1960s. While it was slow but it was steady. America took a decision to withdraw in its involvement in the Vietnam War under President Johnson. China believed this was an indication that the US did not care about Asian expansions. However China began to see that the USSR as a greater threat, especially following the Sino-Soviet border dispute.

It was the People's Republic of China recognized its isolation from the world at a diplomatic level and believed that a better relationship to the US could help. The US could serve as an alternative against China's Soviet threat. It was decided from US officials in the United States to relax the trade restrictions that are imposed on China as well as other obstacles in bilateral relations.

A significant milestone in the development of the relationship occurred in 1971 , when Richard Nixon became the very first US President to visit China. People's Republic of China. It would be several years before the relationship was improved to the point of being normal.

The current state of US and China Relations

In the present it is both the People's Republic of China and the United States share a relationship that is very similar to the relationships between the major European powerhouses at the height of the colonial era. Both countries do trade and share a variety of concerns. But there isn't much trust between the two countries. Both countries have the most powerful economies worldwide. Their financial and trading relation is so that it could influence and even shape the world's economy.

As it happens it is true that the positions between China and the United States and China differ and often clash on international policies and national security questions. There are differences between the two countries at a fundamental level regarding how best to deal with certain states, such as North Korea and Syria. In contrast to those in the US, China is not particularly concerned with the spread and the proliferation in nuclear arsenals. Both countries do not disagree on human rights either. China remains an absolute dictatorship, with total control and the power is vested in the Communist Party. People living in China don't have a wide range of rights.

Chapter 15: Prehistory

Paleolithic Age

What we call China was once the domain of Homo erectus over one million years ago. Late examination demonstrates that the stone instruments found at Xiaochangliang site are magnetostratigraphically dated to 1.36 million years prior. Archeological sites like Xihoudu located in Shanxi Province is the soonest known evidence of the use of fire by Homo erectus. It can be dated 1.27 million years earlier. The excavations in Yuanmou along with later Lantian are evidence of early residence. The most famous instance of Homo erectus discovered within China is the so-called Peking Man found in 1923between 1923 and 27. Fossilized teeth from Homo sapiens dating back to 125,000-80,000 BC have been discovered within Fuyan Cave in Dao County in Hunan.

Neolithic Age

The Neolithic time period of China can be traced through to the time of around 10,000 BC.

The earliest evidence of proto-Chinese millet farming was radiocarbon-dated around 7000 BC. The earliest confirmation of the development of rice, as found in the Yangtze River, is cell base dated to 8,000 year earlier. Growing rice was a way to ascend towards those of Jiahu tradition (7000 until 5800 BC). In Damaidi in Ningxia 3172 precipice carvings dating to 6000to 5500 BC were discovered, "including 8,453 individual characters such as the moon, sun and stars, divine beings and scenes of touching or chasing". The pictographs are believed to be some of the most precise characters and confirmed to be written in Chinese. Chinese proto-composition was present in Jiahu approximately the year 7000 BC, Dadiwan from 5800 BC to 5400 BC Damaidi in the 6000 BC and Banpo that dates back to the fifth millennium BC. Some scholars have suggested to suggest that Jiahu pictures (seventh year BC) represented the earliest Chinese writing framework. Excavating of the Peiligang site of culture in the Xinzheng region in Henan discovered a population which flourished from 5,500 to 4,900 BC and had evidence of agriculture, built stoneware structures, as well as interment of dead. Agribusiness brought increased population as well as the capacity to store and distribute crops and also the opportunity to assist the masters and supervisors. In the latter part of Neolithic conditions it was there was a time when the Yellow River valley started to develop into the focal location for the Yangshao cultural practices (5000 BC to 3000 BC) and the main towns were established. The most archeologically significant of them was located in Banpo, Xi'an. Then, Yangshao culture was superseded by the Longshan culture, which also centered around its Yellow River from around 3000 BC until 2000 BC.

Bronze Age

Bronze rare finds were discovered in The Majiayao Culture site (in the region between 3100 and 2700 BC), The Bronze Age is also mentioned in The

Lower Xiajiadian civilization (22001200 – 1500 BC) site in the upper east China. Sanxingdui located in the currently Sichuan region is believed as the location of a notable ancient city, belonging to previously mysterious Bronze Age culture (in the between 1200 and 2000 BC). The first time the site was discovered was in 1929 and was found in 1986, it was rediscovered in. Chinese archeologists have identified the Sanxingdui culture as part of the ancient kingdom of Shu and have linked the ancient rare finds at the site to the earliest lords of the kingdom.

Chapter 16: Ancient China

Xia regime (2070to 1600 BC)

The Xia administration of China (from about. 2070 until c. 1600 BC) is the main story to be told in chronicled books from the past such as the Sima Qian's Records of the Grand Historian and Bamboo Annals.

The tradition was thought of as legend by historians until the time when archaeological excavations revealed the existence of earlier Bronze Age locales at Erlitou, Henan in 1959. Although there aren't any clear documents describing with the Shang prophet's remains, it remains unclear whether these locations are remaining remnants that belong to the Xia tradition or a different cultural group from the same period. Excavated remains from the tense time period of the Xia show a kind of socially similar groups of chiefdoms. Early marks from this time discovered on shells and ceramics can be believed to be a genealogical link up to the present Chinese characters.

According to historical reports, the administration ended in the year 1600 BC in the aftermath of the battle of Mingtiao.

Shang administration (1600- 1046 BC)

Archeological evidence that proves the existence in Shang line Shang line, which dates from c. 1600-1046 BC can be separated from two groups. The primary set, which dates back to the earlier Shang time frame, is derived from sources in Erligang, Zhengzhou, and Shangcheng. Another set which dates back to the second Shang and Yin (Yin) time frame is located in Anyang located in the province of Henan and is believed to be the last of the Shang's 9 capitals (c. 1300 1046 BC). The finds at Anyang include the most accurate recorded account of Chinese past that has been discovered in the form of divination-related engravings in the old Chinese compositions on bone or the shells from creaturesthe so-called "prophet bones" which date from about 1500 BC.

31 rulers reigned over 31 rulers who ruled over Shang tradition. During their reign as outlined in the Records of the Grand Historian Capital city of Shang had to be relocated six times. The final (and most important) shift was made to Yin the year 1350 BC which led to the administration's stunning time. This phrase Yin Administration has been associated to the Shang line for a long time regardless of the recent fact that it's been used to refer to the last half that are part of Shang tradition. Shang tradition.

Chinese historians who lived in later times were aware of the idea of one tradition being able to succeed another, but the actual political situation in the early China is thought to have been much more involved. Therefore, as some experts of China suggest that it is possible that the Xia along with the Shang may refer to political aspects that were present at the same time, just as the earlier Zhou is believed to exist in the same time with the Shang.

Although the records that were found in Anyang prove the existence that belong to Shang administration. Shang government, Western researchers are frequently not inclined to link settlements which are contemporaneous to the Anyang settlement to those of the Shang line. As an example, archaeological findings at Sanxingdui offer an intriguingly accelerated advancement that is not socially comparable to Anyang. There is no way of showing what extent the Shang domain strayed from Anyang. The most popular hypothesis is that Anyang was managed by a similar Shang during the formal record, existed in conjunction with and exchanged with different settlements that were socially diverse within the region that is now referred in the present as China legitimate.

Zhou regime (1046- Zhou administration (1046-256 BC)

The Zhou administration (1046 BC to roughly 256 BC) was the longest-running line of Chinese history. Prior to the end of the second millennium BC the Zhou administration began to expand within the Yellow River valley, overwhelming the territory that was the Shang. The Zhou appeared to have begun their rule within a semi-primitive framework. The Zhou resided just west of the Shang in addition, the Zhou pioneer was named Western Protector by the Shang. The chief of the Zhou Wu, the King Wu with the aid of his younger brother Duke of Zhou Duke of Zhou as official, came up with a way to defeat the Shang in the Battle of Muye.

The Lord of Zhou has as of today came up with the notion that he had The Mandate of Heaven to legitimize his authority, a notion that is a strong argument for all subsequent traditions. As with Shangdi, Heaven (tian) was the supreme ruler of all gods, and decided who would rule China. It was believed that a ruler would lose their Mandate of Heaven when cataclysmic incidents occurred in an extraordinary amount and they did, the more so the ruler had clearly abandoned his concern for the population at large. The illustrious home would fall and a new house was to take over, given to the Mandate of Heaven.

The Zhou initially moved their capital westwards to a region near to the present-day Xi'an situated in the Wei River, a tributary of the Yellow River, yet they were able to manage a succession of excursions to in the Yangtze River valley. This was the first of many populace moves from the north to the south throughout Chinese time.

The Autumn and Spring seasons (722to 476 BC)

In the 8th century BC the control of the empire was evidently decentralized in the Spring and Autumn period, which was named after the powerful Spring as well as Autumn Annals. At this time, local military pioneers employed by the Zhou began to declare their strength and fight to be kings. The situation was made worse by the attacks of various people groups from northwest, such as the Qin which forced the Zhou to relocate their capital to the east of

Luoyang. This is the second phase of Zhou administration that is known as Zhou's Eastern. Eastern Zhou. The period between the seasons of Spring and Autumn is separated by breaking up of the main Zhou control. In all the states that eventually were created, the local strongmen had the most political power, and continued to exercise their subordination to Zhou rulers, and in practice. A few of the pioneers from the neighborhood even adopted prestigious names for themselves. China now comprises a number of states, with some similar to the town that has an enclave.

The time passed and larger and more powerful states were joined or were guaranteed suzerainty over smaller ones. At the end of the sixth century BC the majority of small states had ceased to be connected and only a handful of powerful and efficient states controlled China. Some states in the south like Chu and Wu granted freedom from the Zhou who fought wars against a few of their own (Wu as well as Yue). Many modern urban zones were set during this time and Chinese culture gradually developed.

While all of these powerful leaders had settled solidly in their own areas, the massacre was focused entirely on interstate conflicts during the Warring States time frame, that began when three outstanding elite families from the Jin state three families - Zhao, Wei and Han split the state. Many well-known people, like Lao Zi, Confucius and Sun Tzu lived amid this turbulent period.

The Hundred Schools of Thought of Chinese theory flourished during this time, and powerful scholarly ideas like Confucianism Taoism, Legalism and Mohism were established, largely due to the shifting political environment. The first two philosophical thoughts had a profound influence upon Chinese culture.

Warring States period (476- 221 BC)

Following further consolidation of the political system seven states were able to remain until the fifth century's end BC and the time during which these states competed against with each other are called The Warring States time frame. While there was an apparent Zhou leader until the year 256 BC but he was mostly an unimportant entity and had no actual authority.

Chapter 17: Imperial China

Northern and Southern dynasties (AD 589 - 420)

In the middle of the fifth century China was thrown into a period called the Northern and Southern dynasties. During this time, separate administrations ruled both Northern and Southern areas of the country. In the south they were known as the Eastern Jin offered route to the Liu Song, Southern Qi, Liang lastly Chen. The three Southern Dynasties were driven by Han Chinese decision families and employed Jiankang (current Nanjing) as the capital. They fended off attacks from the north and protected various aspects of Chinese human development, as northern savage regimes began to become sinful.

To the North, the rest of the Sixteen Kingdoms was stifled in 439 by the Northern Wei, a kingdom created by the Xianbei wandering people who joined northern China. It was then that the Northern Wei inevitably split into the Eastern and Western Wei, which at time turned into Northern Qi and Northern Zhou. The administrations were led through Xianbei as well as Han Chinese who had hitched to Xianbei families. In this time, the majority of Xianbei people received Han surnames, at the end, causing complete digestion of the Han.

Despite the nation's divide, Buddhism spread all through the nation. In the southern part of China there were a lot of tense discussions on whether Buddhism should be permitted were discussed all the time by the royal courts and the nobles. At the time of the period Buddhists and Taoists have proven to be tolerant of one another.

Northern and Southern dynasties (AD 589 - 420)

In the middle of the five hundred years, China was undergoing a transition called the Northern and Southern customs, where two administrations were in charge of the northern and southern regions of the country. In the south it was known as the Eastern Jin offered path to the Liu Song, Southern Qi, Liang lastly Chen. The three Southern Dynasties were driven by Han Chinese decision families and used Jiankang (present present day Nanjing) as their capital. They were able to fend off attacks from the north, and also protected various parts of Chinese development and the northern brutal administrations began to sinify.

To the North, the rest of the Sixteen Kingdoms was quenched in 439 by the Northern Wei, a kingdom created by the Xianbei who were a people of migrant origin who brought north and southern China. It was the Northern Wei in the long run was split into Eastern as well as the Western Wei, which at this point became the Northern Qi and Northern Zhou. The ruling administrations were led by Xianbei or Han Chinese who had hitched to Xianbei families. In the period, most Xianbei people embraced Han surnames, and in the end, they were forced to total enslavement to the Han.

In spite of the divisions within this
nation Buddhism has spread across the
country. In the southern part of China
there were savage disputes regarding
whether Buddhism should be permitted
were scheduled occasionally by the
royal courts and the nobles. Prior to the
end of the period Buddhists and Taoists
have proven to be much more accepting
of one another.

Sui dynasty (581- 618)

The dynasty line, which was brief, was a
crucial time of Chinese history. The Sui
was founded by the Emperor Wen in
581 as a progress from the Northern
Zhou, the Sui was able to defeat
China's Southern Chen in 589 to unify
China and end three years of political
conflict. The Sui established a number
of new institutions that included the
administration structure comprised of
Three Departments and Six Ministries
magnificent examinations to select
individuals from the general population
as well as enhancing the fubing
frameworks of the induction of armed

forces and the Equal-field system of land allocations. These tactics were accepted by the later traditions, led to massive population growth and added unneeded wealth to the state. Coinage was formally recognized throughout the entire world. Buddhism was a prominent faith and was recognized as a formal. Sui China was known for its numerous super-development projects. It was proposed for grain transportation and transportation of troops and troops, and for transporting troops, the Grand Canal was developed, connecting the capital cities Daxing (Chang'an) as well as Luoyang to the secluded southeast region, and in a different direction, towards the east's upper fringe. It was also the case that the Great Wall was likewise extended and a series of military victories and conciliatory movements also calmed its borders. However the massive attacks on Korea's Korean Peninsula amid the GoguryeoSui War were tragically bombed and triggered a variety of rebellions that led to the abolition of the old tradition.

Tang dynasty (AD 618- 907)

Many Chinese adhere to the Tang Dynasty (618-907) to be the highest goal of Imperial China as a whole, both politically as well as socially. The empire reached its greatest size prior to it was ruled by the Manchu Qing Dynasty, turning into the center for the East Asian world connected by content, religion, and various political and financial establishments. Additionally, Tang essayists deliver the best verses of China's amazing verse convention.

The Tang tradition was founded by the Emperor Gaozu on June 18, 618. It was an era of Chinese human development and believed to have been the best period of China with significant advancements in the arts of craftsmanship, culture writing, particularly poetry, and invention. Buddhism became the dominant religion of the common people. Chang'an (present present day Xi'an) which is the nation's capital, was once the biggest city in the world at the present time.

The second ruler, Taizong, is broadly considered to be one of the most powerful heads in Chinese history. He set the stage to allow the line to flourish for a considerable period after his reign. The consolidated military successes as well as political actions were implemented to eliminate threats from clans that traveled, widen the frontier, and enslave the neighboring states to an tributary structure. The military victories within the Tarim Basin kept the Silk Road open, linking Chang'an with Central Asia and zones far towards the west. South of the river, the lucrative sea exchange programs began from urban ports such as Guangzhou. There was a wide exchange of information with distant nations and a variety of dealers established themselves in China creating a multi-cultural cultural. The Tang cultural and social structures were observed and emulated by other nations, the particularly Japan. Within the Grand Canal connected the political center of Chang'an to the financial and rural focuses in the southern and eastern regions of the region.

The secret to the success in the beginning of the Tang lines was the existence of a sturdy unit with a well-organized approach. The administration was organized in "Three departments and Six Ministries" to independently make, examine and execute arrangements. These offices were overseen by royal relatives, and also research authorities, who were chosen through a series of regal tests. These customs, which were developed within the Tang tradition, were followed in the following lines with some minor changes.

In the Tang "measure as high as deal with framework" the entire property was claimed by the Emperor and given to the individual as per the estimates of family units. The men who were allowed to arrive to be drafted into military administration for a fixed period each year, which was a strategy for military called"the "Fubing Framework". These arrangements led to rapid increase in efficiency and led to an armed force that was crucial, without any burden on the state's Treasury. At the time of the midpoint of the tradition, it was clear that standing forces of armed force had replaced induction and land was always under the control of private owners.

The tradition continued to grow under the aegis of the Empress Wu Zetian, the main ruler of the regnant era in Chinese time, and reached its height under the reign of Emperor Xuanzong who was the ruler of an area that stretched all the way from Pacific up to the Aral Sea with no less than 50 million inhabitants. There were numerous cultural and political manifestations, which included the works of two top Chinese authors, Li Bai, and Du Fu.

The peak of the prosperity of the kingdom, A Lushan Rebellion from 755 to 763 was a pivotal moment that devastated the people and weakened the powerful government. In the endless supply of defiance local military governors called Jiedushi, took gradually independent status. In the absence of revenue from the arrival impose the focal government was heavily dependent on salt syndicating. At a distance, the meek states of earlier took on the domain and the vast fringe regions were lost as a result of centuries. However, the general society recovered and prospered the midst of a degraded great structure.

In the late Tang period the Tang period was characterized by incompetent and corrupt rulers and officials at the supreme court that allowed local warlords to cause generalized rebellions. The most disastrous one was Huang Chao Rebellion, from 874 to 884. It affected the entire world for a period of 10 years. The devastation of the port in the south Guangzhou which occurred in the year 879 followed by the massacre of the majority of its inhabitants, as well as the vast enclaves of traders in remote areas. In 881, the two capital cities, Luoyang and Chang'an, declined gradually. Their dependence upon the ethnic Han or Turkic warlords to stifle the subordination of their people increased their strength and influence. Then, the fall of the line in the wake of Zhu Wen's usurpation led to an era of disintegration.

Five Dynasties and Ten Kingdoms (AD 907-960)

The period of political unrest in China's Tang as well as the Song often referred to as the Five Dynasties and Ten Kingdoms period, lasted between 907 and 996. Through this period, China was in all regards a multi-state structure. Five administrations, in particular, (Later) Liang, Tang, Jin, Han and Zhou swiftly succeeded each other in the responsibility of the standard Imperial central region in the northern part of China. In the various administrations, the leaders from (Later) Tang, Jin and Han were sinicized Shatuo Turks, which administered the largest share of the ethnicity of Han Chinese. The more stable and less centralized administrations that were largely ethnic Han rulers were in place in the western and southern regions of China during the time, and in total, they formed"the "Ten kingdoms".

In the midst of a political conflict in the north, the Sixteen Prefectures (district along the current Great Wall) were surrendered to the emerging Khitan Liao Dynasty, which severely weakened the China right against the northern wandering realms. To to the South Vietnam expanded its autonomy as a result of being an independent Chinese prefecture for a lengthy period of. When wars were raging within Northern China, there were large-scale southward movements of people that also accelerated the southward shift of financial and social focuses in China. The time culminated by the saga that occurred under Later Zhou general Zhao Kuangyin and the founding of in 960. Song regime in 960. This was to eventually destroy the remaining regions from China's "Ten Kingdoms" and then reunified China.

Song, Liao, Jin along with Western Xia dynasties (AD 960 1234)

In the year 960 In 960, in 960, the Song line of succession was initiated by the Emperor Taizu and its capital being established in Kaifeng (otherwise known as Bianjing). In 979 the Song tradition brought together the vast majority of China legal, although large portions of the external domains were held of sinicized kingdoms. In 979, the Khitan Liao Administration, which continued between 907 and 1125 ruled in Manchuria, Mongolia, and portions from Northern China. Between the years in the present the north-western Chinese regions comprising Gansu, Shaanxi, and Ningxia the Tangut clans created an administration called the Western Xia administration from 1032 until 1227.

In hopes of regaining the vital Sixteen Prefectures that were lost under the previous administration, crusades were launched against Liao tradition during the early Song time period, and ended in disappointment. In 1004, at that time it was the time that the Liao rangers cleared the unexplored North China Plain and achieved the borders of Kaifeng which forced the Song's concession and later agreement to the Chanyuan Treaty, which forced significant annual tributes from the Song Treasury. This arrangement was an important change in the Chinese force of the traditional framework for tributary. The annual pouring out of Song's silver into the Liao was repaid by the purchase of Chinese goods and products that boosted the Song economy and refilled its Treasury. This was the trigger to the Song to also fight the Liao. Between then the cross-fringe exchange as well as contact further accelerated sinicization in the Liao Empire and to the negative effect on its military might that resulted from its primitive way of living. Social-sparing and bargaining agreements were observed in Song's relationships with Jin. Jin line.

In the Liao Empire In the Liao Empire, the Jurchen clans protested against their lords in order to create their own Jin Line in the year 1115. In 1125 the overwhelming Jin cataphract wiped out the Liao line, and the remaining of Liao court officials went to Central Asia to establish the Qara Khitai Empire (Western Liao Dynasty). Jin's assault on the Song tradition followed swiftly. After 1127 Kaifeng fell, the most devastating disaster, known as The Jingkang Incident, finishing the Northern Song

Dynasty. In the following years, the whole northern part of China was conquered. The remaining individuals of the Song court were reunited in the capital of Hangzhou and established with the Southern Song tradition, which was the rule of domains that were that were south of Huai River. In the years following the populace and the domain of China were divided from the Song administration and the Jin tradition. Jin tradition, and the Western Xia line. The period was concluded with the Mongol victory and the Mongol victory, as Western Xia fell in 1227 Then the Jin administration was in 1234, and then it was the Southern Song tradition in 1279.

Despite its weaknesses in military in the military, this Song line is generally believed to be the primary goal of the traditional Chinese development. In the Song economy, spurred by advancement in innovation reached a point of refinement that is likely to be invisible to the world at this point. is the best moment. The population increased to over 100 million, and expectations for daily comforts for average people increased significantly due to advancements in rice development and the availability of coal to generate. The capital city communities of Kaifeng and Hangzhou were the two most crowded cities in the world to their potential and facilitated active social systems that were which were not matched by the previous Chinese customs. Since land exchange routes to the further west were blocked by realms that traveled around as well as the wide oceanic exchanges with states that were neighboring that encouraged the use of Song coins as the preferred currency for trade. Massive wooden vessels equipped with compasses travelled across in the China Seas and northern Indian Ocean. The concept of protecting was practiced by shippers to help mitigate the risk of these shipping by sea. Thanks to the success of financial transactions the first use of cash on paper was discovered in the west of Chengdu in addition to the existing copper coins.

The Song Dynasty was thought to be the golden era of amazing advancements in science and technological innovation in China because of innovative researchers, like such as Su Song (1020- 1101) and Shen Kuo (1031- 1095). Innovative inventions, such as the galactic clock made of hydro-mechanical technology, the most enduring and continuous chain of influence transmission as well as woodblock printing and paper cash were all invented during the Song Dynasty.

There was a court battle between political reformers and the preservationists, pushed by chancellors Wang Anshi and Sima Guang both separately. In the late thirteenth century the Chinese had adopted the orthodox Neo-Confucian theories formulated through Zhu Xi. The most epic artistic works were included within the Song administration, such as the chronicled work called the Zizhi Tongjian ("Comprehensive Mirror to aid in the Administration"). The advent of mobile printing also facilitated the spread of education. Human expressions and culture thrived through vainglorious works of art like the River Along the River During the Qingming Festival and the Eighteen Songs of a Nomad Flute along with amazing Buddhist artists like the prolific Lin Tinggui.

The Song administration was also an era of the greatest growth ever. The development of black powder during the Tang Dynasty, was first utilized in areas of combat by the Song Armed Force, which prompted an increase in the number of guns and attack motors ' outlines. The Southern Song Dynasty, as its future depended on defending the Yangtze and Huai River against the rangers power from north, the main remaining naval strength in China was gathered in 1132. Its the chief of naval operations' command centrally set in Dinghai. Warships equipped with Oar Wheels and Trebuchets could launch combustible explosives composed of lime and explosives as documented in Song's victory over the aggressive Jin forces during the Battle of Tangdao in the East China Sea, and the Battle of Caishi on the Yangtze River in 1161.

The progress in development during the Song line came to an abrupt end with the massive Mongol victory, during which the population slowed and a massive contraction in the economy. Despite having violently ended Mongol development for three years in the region, the Southern Song capital Hangzhou fell in 1276. It was followed by the final annihilation by the Song standing naval force during the Battle of Yamen in 1279.

Yuan dynasty (AD 1271- 1368)

The Yuan Dynasty was formally declared in 1271. It was when the Great Khan of Mongol, Kublai Khan, one of Genghis Khan's grandsons was hoping to be granted the title of Emperor of China and contemplated his new piece from the Mongol Empire as an Chinese Dynasty. In the past it was believed that the Mongols were able to defeat their enemies in the Jin Dynasty in Northern China as well as their Southern Song administration fell in 1279 after a lengthy and bloody conflict. In 1279, the Mongol Yuan Dynasty turned into the primary success line in Chinese history, governing the entirety of China in its entirety and its population in the form of an ethnic minorities. The government also ruled the Mongolian central region and other regions which included the most lucrative deal of an area within the divided Mongol Empire. It generally was in agreement with the most cutting-edge area of China and adjoining districts in East Asia. The Assist expansion of the realm was ended in the aftermath of annihilation during the wars of Japan as well as Vietnam. As a result of the former Jin Dynasty, the capital of the Yuan Dynasty was built up in Khanbaliq (otherwise known as Dadu which is cutting-edge Beijing). In the Grand Canal, the Grand Canal was reproduced to link the capital city's remote location with financial centers in the the southern region of China and set the priorities and setting the place the location where Beijing will remain as the capital city of the progressive administrations that bind together China the territory.

After the peace deal in 1304 that ended the progression of Mongols common wars, the leaders of the Yuan Dynasty were maintained as the presumed the Great Khan (Khagan) of the more notable Mongol Empire against other Mongol Khanates that was deemed to be to be self-ruling. The period was called Pax Mongolica, when a large portion in the Asian mainland was governed under the control of Mongols. For the first time the silk street was completely controlled by a single state that encouraged the flow of exchange between individuals and social commerce. Systems of streets and a postal frameworks were established to connect the vast domain. The lucrative oceanic exchange, originating in the past Song Dynasty, kept on flourishing, and Quanzhou and Hangzhou emerged as the largest ports in the world. The most shrewd travelers from the west, including Marco Polo, the Venetian, Marco Polo, could have settled in China for a considerable period of. After his arrival and his detailed travel diary inspired the ages of medieval Europeans and influenced the traits of the far east. It was believed that the Yuan Dynasty was the primary old economic system, and paper cash, also known in the past as Chao was used as the ultimate medium for trade. The unlimited supply of paper currency during the latter days of the Yuan administration led to hyperinflation that eventually caused the demise of this line.

Although those who were Mongol rulers from the Yuan Dynasty embraced generously to Chinese cultural traditions but their sinicization was of a lesser significance compared to prior victory lines in Chinese the past. To preserve racial dominance as the victor and the decision group, traditional roaming tradition and the legacy of to the Mongolian steppe were regarded with reverence. However the Mongol rulers also were able to adapt to the diverse societies from a variety of propelled changes within the vast realm. Traditional social structure and cultural practices in China changed dramatically during the Mongol power. There was a significant number of transients from distant countries who settled in China who benefited from a higher prosperity over the predominant part of Han Chinese, while improving Chinese culture by incorporating elements from outside. The research authorities and educated people, traditional holders of top Chinese culture, lost their generous social status. This encouraged the growth of the culture of ordinary people. The works were a success that were performed in zaju theater and scholarly tunes (sanqu) composed by a group of musicians written in a specific form of verse called qu. The vernacular style books increased the awe-inspiring status and popularity. In fact, the first three of these fantastic published books were created during the period of change in administration between Yuan and Ming Dynasties.

In the days prior to Mongol assault, Chinese traditions announced around 120 million tenants. When the triumph was completed by 1279 enumeration of 1300 identified around 60 million. This decline isn't solely due to Mongol murders. For instance, researchers like Frederick W. Bit contend that the large decline in population is a result of an inability to accurately record the actual decline other researchers, such as, Timothy Brook contend that the Mongols were able to arrange the enserfment of a large portion of the Chinese population, causing many to disappear from the enumeration both from the inside out. Other antiquarians like William McNeill and David Morgan believe that torture was the primary reason behind the decline in the number of people recorded during the period. In the 14th century, China suffered from more devastating plagues of torture, estimated to have killed 25 million people, or 30% of the total number of inhabitants living in China.

Through the Yuan administration there was a general idea among the population in opposition to Mongol dominance. But instead of the patriotism it was mainly a string of catastrophic events and inadequacy government that ignited endless worker revolts from the 1340s onwards. After the huge maritime battle in Lake Poyang, Zhu Yuanzhang defeated other rebel powers in the south. He declared his sovereignty and founded his own Ming Dynasty in 1368. The year was 1368 when his northern campaign's armed forces captured Khanbaliq, the capital of Khanbaliq. The Yuan remaining Yuan escaped back to Mongolia and ran the government. There were other Mongol Khanate in Central Asia kept on existing after the end of the Yuan customs in China.

Ming dynasty (AD 1368- 1644)

The Ming administration was founded through Zhu Yuanzhang in 1368, who declared himself"the" Hongwu Emperor. The capital was initially located in Nanjing before being transferred to Beijing after the Yongle Emperor's rule .

Urbanization grew exponentially as the population increased, and the work division became more fascinating. Large urban centers like Nanjing and Beijing also contributed to the rise of private sector. Particularly, small scale enterprises emerged, usually with an understanding of cotton, silk, paper and porcelain items. In general, however, moderately tiny cities have businesses that are spread across the country. The town is mainly an exchange for food and some essential products such as stick or even oil.

The xenophobia, and the academic reflections that are typical of the well-known new school of neo-Confucianism China in the first Ming time period wasn't completely isolated. Contacts via remote exchange and other channels with the world outside and especially Japan was booming. Chinese traders explored the entire portion of Indian Ocean, achieving East Africa through the travels that of Zheng He.

Hongwu Emperor, the primary ancestor of Chinese practices from the laborer's beginning point, established the structure of an express, which relied on farming in general. Exchange and business were flourishing in previous Song as well as Yuan patterns, was not as and less emphasized. The land holdings of the Neo-medieval Song and Mongol period were confiscated by Ming rulers. Land bequests were distributed through the legislative branch, split and then the land was leased. Private subjection was a crime. So, after the fall of the Yongle Emperor, independent workers were the dominant landowners in Chinese Agribusiness. These laws could have been a way to eliminate the most poor of the neediness of the administrations of the past. In the later years in the Ming administration, there was a decrease in government control exchange, business and private companies were revived.

The line was a strong and intricate focal administration that linked and controlled the whole realm. The head's position was more oppressive despite being able to Hongwu Emperor continued using what he called"the "Terrific Secretariat" to aid in the huge printed documents from the administrative branch, such as the remembrances (petitions and applications to the prestigious position) as well as amazing orders to answer to various reports as well as expense reports. This same administration that prevented from the Ming government from being able to change with the changes in the public's view and eventually caused its decline.

The Yongle Emperor fought hard to increase China's influence past its borders by having various rulers send envoys to China to offer a an homage. A massive naval force was created comprising four-masted boats that could dislodge 1,500 tons. A standing force with 1 million soldiers (some measure at 1.9 million) was created. The Chinese army defeated and controlled Vietnam for about 20 years. The Chinese armies cruised the China oceans as well as in the Indian Ocean, cruising similar to the eastern shoreline of Africa. The Chinese made an impact in the eastern part of Moghulistan. A handful of oceanic Asian countries sent emissaries in an ode to China's sovereign. Chinese sovereign. Locally there was a Grand Canal was extended and was transformed into a boost to residential exchange. The iron equivalent of more than 100,000 tonnes each year were shipped. A lot of books were printed using the portable sort. The royal palace of the highest rank at Beijing's Forbidden City has reached its current splendor. It was also during the past a hundred years that the capacity of south China became totally used to its fullest. New harvests were extensively established and ventures, like for instance, those that produced materials and porcelain, prospered.

In 1449, Esen Tayisi led in 1449 an Oirat Mongol intrusion of northern China that culminated with the capture of the Zhengtong the Emperor in Tumu. From then on the Ming advanced towards being on edge in the northern edges and led to for the Ming Great Wall being assembled. The majority of what is left in today's Great Wall of China today was built or restored during the Ming. The rock and block work was expanded, the watchtowers were improved, and guns were installed across the length of the wall.

The Adrift Ming became increasingly independent after the departure of Yongle Emperor. The fortune-seekers that cruised the Indian Ocean were stopped, and Sea denial law was put in place to prohibit the Chinese from traveling across the oceans. European merchants who landed in China in the Age of Discovery were over and over criticized in their requests for exchange, and the Portuguese being rejected at the hands of Ming military during Tuen Mun in 1521 and the same thing happened in 1522. Remote and local requests for exchange with foreign countries considered illegal by the government, caused widespread wokou thefts that ravaged the coastline in the southeastern region under the control that was imposed by Jiajing Emperor (15071507 - 1567) that was slain in the wake of the opening of port facilities in Guangdong and Fujian and a lot of military cover-up. The Portuguese were allowed to establish themselves within Macau in 1557 in exchange for trade and remained in Portuguese control until the year 1999. The Dutch portion of China's Chinese oceans was also greeted by a fierce protection, the Dutch being chased by the Penghu islands during the Sino-Dutch conflict in 1622-1624. They were forced to relocate to Taiwan. Taiwan was the home of Dutch. Dutch in Taiwan engaged with the Ming during 1633 at the Battle of Liaoluo Bay in 1633 and were defeated, and then eventually surrendered to Ming adherent Koxinga in 1662, following the demise of the Ming customs.

In 1556, under the control that was imposed by Jiajing Emperor in 1556, the Shaanxi earthquake killed 830,000 people, making it the deadliest earthquake ever.

The Ming dynasty played a significant role during the Japanese invasions into Korea (1592-98) and ended with the surrender of all hostile Japanese power in Korea as well as the restitution of the Joseon line, which was its traditional partner and state of tributary. The local government that was part of Ming was saved. Ming Administration was restored from the cost of its assets. Furthermore, under Ming's supervision in Manchuria declining and the Manchu (Jurchen) clans under the leadership of their chieftain Nurhaci separated from the Ming standard and emerged as an abrasive and bound-together state which was later broadcast under The Qing line. The line was used to suppress the debilitated Korea as its tributary defeated Mongolia and expanded its territory all the way to the edge Great Wall.

www.ingramcontent.com/pod-product-compliance
Lightning Source LLC
Chambersburg PA
CBHW050401120526
44590CB00015B/1780